TWTTL

(The Way, The Truth, and The Life)

*...offering a concise installment in a
timely and timeless line of inquiry...*

TWTTTL

(The Way, The Truth, and The Life)

**A Guide to the *Ultimate Fullness*
of Meaning and Fulfillment**

An LJ2025 publication

Published by LJ2025 Publishing
Pennsylvania, USA
www.lj2025.org

Front and Back Cover photo: *"Lighthouse-coast-sea-tower"* via Pixabay
Cover and Interior by LJ2025 Publishing
979-8-9866030-8-7 eBook 3rd edition.
979-8-9866030-7-0 paperback 3rd edition.

Table of Contents - Summary

Table of Figures

Introduction

"He is the Way, the Truth, and the Life; that is,
the Bridge which leads you to the height of Heaven."
— St. Catherine of Siena

Vast libraries of materials have been produced over the centuries to describe mankind's understanding of themselves as living creatures in the universe, its origins (and ours), the possibility of a creator-God, the nature of our relationship to such, and our ultimate destiny.

This offering, while not-so-humble in its subject and scope, humbly attempts to provide a brief listing of answers to these fundamental questions in concise terms and in a set of direct statements consistent with an essentially Judeo-Christian perspective. It further attempts to do so in a 'top-down' approach so the essence of it can be scanned at a glance, the substance of it reviewed in a few minutes, the text of it read in several sittings, and the depth of it plumbed to whatever extent desired.

The result sketches an outline of understanding that can be presented to any and all for consideration. The aim is not to give a 'proof', nor a 'pro and con' discussion or debate, but to simply lay out in 'cheat-sheet' fashion an integrated way of seeing things that is self-consistent, rational, reasonable, accessible, and which points to supporting information and references available to explore according to interest and inclination.

In the past, popular as well as scholarly critiques to these kinds of ideas have been put forward, perhaps even more so in recent times. And while many of the underlying references deal specifically with some of those challenges, the intent is not to directly engage them here. Instead, it is to offer an alternative view – "the other side of the story" – and, in doing so, bring insights to typical misunderstandings or misconceptions that can sometimes get in the way of openness to a more balanced and even-handed approach to the questions at hand. The guide further presents a collection of supplementary reference materials which stands in answer to the often-made assertion of 'no evidence' in support of these ideas and the beliefs which naturally flow from them.

With no apology or reservation, the statements listed in this discussion are suggested as demonstrable and objective realities which are not dependent on our subjective acceptance or belief; it is up to each individual reader to determine for themselves whether to receive them in that light. If nothing else, those who yet remain skeptical will at least have had the opportunity to become aware of background and corresponding source materials they may not have otherwise known to exist. It is then hoped such a determination can be well (or at least better) informed as a result.

Whatever the outcome, if the take-away impressions from this reading include things like "there's more to that than I realized...", "I never heard that before...", "that seems to make sense...", or "I never thought of it that way...", then this effort will have been worthwhile on both ends of the exchange.

Table of Contents - Detail

Overview Summary

3.2.3   He grew to manhood and at the age of thirty began public ministry.

3.2.4   He taught with wisdom and authority.

3.2.5   He performed healings and other miracles.

3.2.6   He fulfilled many prophesies.

3.2.7   He claimed to be the 'Son of God', one with 'God the Father'.

3.2.8   He was accused of blasphemy and opposition to imperial rule, and was put to death.

3.2.9   He rose from the dead on the third day following his death and burial.

3.3   He Left Us Means and a Mission

3.3.1   He appeared to many witnesses for forty days following His resurrection.

3.3.2   He offered the glorious gift of eternal life together with Him and God the Father.

3.3.3   He described the dim alternative of eternal life separated from Him and God the Father.

3.3.4   He founded a Church as a means for us to be healed and reconciled to Him and to all.

3.3.5   He promised to return at the end of time.

3.3.6   He promised to send us His Spirit for guidance and support in the interim.

3.3.7   He authorized & sent His followers to teach, heal, minister, and call others in His name.

3.3.8   He promised to be with them until the end of time.

3.3.9   He ascended and disappeared into the sky.

4 The Legacy

4.1   The Message (What did He teach?)

4.1.1   Summary of His Teachings – Love God, Love Your Neighbor as Yourself

4.1.2   Highlights of His Teachings – Parables, Exhortations, Revelations

4.2   The Medium (Knowing *about* Him)

4.2.1   His legacy of interaction with mankind was compiled and conveyed over millennia.

4.2.2   His legacy was compiled and conveyed initially through oral, and later written means.

4.2.3   His legacy has preserved integrity & coherence via authoritative oversight & guidance.

4.2.4   His legacy has stability which rests upon three supporting elements.

4.2.5   The Church He founded has responsibility and authority to faithfully convey this legacy.

4.3   The Relationship (Knowing Him *personally*)

4.3.1   We come to know Him personally in Prayer (We speak, He listens/He speaks, We listen).

4.3.2   We each pray individually in private, and we all pray together in community.

4.3.3   We grow in relationship with Him one-on-one, and as a body – the Church.

4.3.4   We grow more fully in our identity as 'human person' through this two-fold relationship.

4.3.5   We experience this relationship directly with Him and indirectly through others.

4.3.6   We experience this relationship as both immanent and transcendent to ourselves.

4.3.7   We are transformed & empowered in this relationship, both naturally & supernaturally.

4.3.8   We become one w/Him in Worship & Sacrament (We give,He receives/He gives,We receive).

5 The Direction

5.1   We Follow Him, Become Like Him, and Invite Others to Do the Same

5.1.1   He gives us a perfect model and example to follow.

5.1.2   We grow to be like Him to the extent we respond, engage, & receive all we are given.

5.1.3   We help others by giving to them as we were given to.

5.2   We Seek All That is Of Him (Holiness)

5.2.1   Some spiritual beings (Angels - 7.1.4) accept service to God & support us.

5.2.2   They facilitate influence consistent with God; our cooperation draws us closer to Him.

5.2.3   We are vulnerable on our own, but are promised their assistance, with God's grace.

5.3   We Reject All That is Not Of Him (Evil)

5.3.1   Some spiritual beings (Demons, "fallen angels"-7.1.4) reject service to God & oppose us.

5.3.2   They facilitate influence contrary to God; our cooperation moves us away from Him.

5.3.3   We are vulnerable on our own, but are promised to overcome them, with God's grace.

6 The Path

6.1   Be Open and Grow in Faith, Hope, and Love on the Inside

6.1.1   Know and be known with Him in the silence and intimacy of Prayer

6.1.2   Connect and grow with Him in the depth and richness Scripture

6.1.3   Connect and live with Him in the secure context of Tradition.

6.1.4   Unite & be transformed by Him & His Church in the communion of Worship & Sacrament

6.2   Be Real and Express Faith, Hope, and Love on the Outside
  6.2.1   We offer to others, in service to Him, support of their needs of the body (Corporal Works)
  6.2.2   We offer to others, in service to Him, support of their needs of the soul (Spiritual Works)
  6.2.3   We use sacramentals as tangible reminders and indications of our faith and devotion.
  6.2.4   We invite others to participate in the same fullness of relationship and destiny with God.
6.3   Be Aware of Opposition
  6.3.1   We are subject to deception and response to influence contrary to God.
  6.3.2   We thus contribute to growth of disorder, sin, sickness, & death in material creation.
  6.3.3   We thus contribute to growth of defect, blemish, stain, & corruption in spiritual creation.
  6.3.4   We thus damage and sometimes break our right order of relationship to God & others.
  6.3.5   We experience this challenge of influence contrary to God as life-long struggle.
  6.3.6   We can grow in ability to recognize deception by cooperating with God & His grace.
  6.3.7   We can grow in ability to reject contrary influence by cooperating with God & His grace.
  6.3.8   He gave us a means for reconciling broken relationship through, with, and in His Church.

7 The Support
7.1   Our Mentors and Guardians
  7.1.1   Those human beings who have gone before us & lived exemplary lives are our mentors.
  7.1.2   Some mentors are formally recognized as Saints worthy to admire and aspire to.
  7.1.3   Saints are with God, are for us, and can intercede in prayer on our behalf upon request.
  7.1.4   Angels are spiritual beings created before us who live in service to God, with and for us.
  7.1.5   A specific angel is assigned to each one of us to serve as our guardian throughout our life.
  7.1.6   Angels are with God (thus, also Saints) and can intercede and act on our behalf.
7.2   Our Immediate Family
  7.2.1   Those human beings who are here with us now living are all our brothers and sisters.
  7.2.2   Some brothers and sisters seek to live life in close relationship to God and can assist us.
  7.2.3   We serve God when we seek to live saintly lives bringing others to Him and Him to others.
  7.2.4   The Church is the community in which such saintly lives are encouraged and nourished.
  7.2.5   The Church embodies His Legacy (see 4) and provides us Means in our Mission (see 3.3)
  7.2.6   We thus bring light, love, order, & right relationship into this life & carry it into eternity.
7.3   Our Extended Family
  7.3.1   God came to save all mankind and expressed a desire for unity among all people.
  7.3.2   Influences contrary to God have arisen in history introducing errors in teaching & belief.
  7.3.3   Influences contrary to God have facilitated division, splits, and fragmentation.
  7.3.4   The Church remained essentially one for nearly 1000 years before an East/West break.
  7.3.5   The Church experienced the next major split in the 1500's, first of many continuing today.
  7.3.6   The Church seeks to draw all separated brethren into unity of faith, if not in expression.
  7.3.7   The Church seeks to draw all of mankind into right relationship with God and each other.

8 The Goal
8.1   Wholeness
  8.1.1   We integrate both aspects of our humanity, body & soul, in our expression of life & love.
  8.1.2   We experience wholeness when in alignment with what is true, good, and beautiful.
  8.1.3   We experience fullness of life when we are in right relationship with God and others.
  8.1.4   We find grounding for wholeness and fullness of life in attributes of holiness.
8.2   Peace and Joy
  8.2.1   We experience 'happiness' (i.e., peace & joy), through holiness, right relation with God.
  8.2.2   We experience unfulfillment (i.e., emptiness & angst) in worldly things apart from God.
  8.2.3   We are commonly deceived by counterfeits of power, prestige, pleasure, & possessions.
  8.2.4   We are commonly misled by attractions focused inward on self, vs outward toward others.
8.3   Eternity
  8.3.1   We live life as integrated body & soul, but on death, our soul will separate from the body.
  8.3.2   We will encounter Him at the moment of death and experience our particular judgement.
  8.3.3   We will experience the fullness of God's justice and mercy.
  8.3.4   Our soul will experience an ultimate eternal destiny with God, or separated from Him.
  8.3.5   At the end of time, Jesus will again return to earth for a general judgement of all mankind.
  8.3.6   Our bodies will be resurrected in glorified form and reunited with our soul.

TWTTTL

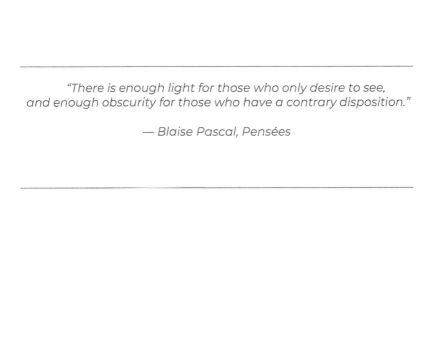

"There is enough light for those who only desire to see, and enough obscurity for those who have a contrary disposition."

— Blaise Pascal, Pensées

1   The Big Picture

In the beginning was the Word, ... and the Word was God...
All things were made through him... In him was life, and the life was the light of men.
The light shines in the darkness, and the darkness has not overcome it.
—— John 1:1-5

There is a God and He loves us.

1.1   There is a God
He is above all and created everything.

1.1.1   He is now, always has been, and always will be.

1.1.2   He is spirit and eternal.

1.1.3   He is being itself.

1.1.4   He is love.

1.1.5   He is creator of all else that is, both spirit and matter.

1.1.6   He is glorious and light is of Him.

Efforts to prove God's existence are bound to be incomplete, since we are considering a transcendent being beyond everything else. The question is not so much "is there proof?", but "is there enough indication of a likelihood, or even a possibility', such that it is reasonable to believe?". [3, 4, 5, 6]

1.2   He is all-goodness, all-truth, all-beauty; all-knowing, all-powerful, and all-present.
He is the highest good, the absolute truth.

1.2.1   He reveals Himself in His creation, within us, in circumstances, and in history.

1.2.2   He has interacted with us and revealed Himself to us gradually over millennia.

1.2.3   He invites all of us and each of us into relationship.

1.2.4   He does not force Himself upon us.

1.2.5   He speaks to us through our mind, heart, imagination, experience, and relationships.

---

[3] Ref 8.1 Cronin, F. (2020). *The World According to God*; Chapters on Matters of Origin, - Order, - Reason
[4] (Ibid) Chapters on Matters of the All, - Divinity, - Proximity and Activity
[5] (Ibid) Chapters on Matters of Revelation
[6] Ref 5.13 Spitzer, F. R. (2017). *Big Book* - Credible Catholic [https://www.crediblecatholic.com/big-book/] - Volume 1 – THE EXISTENCE OF GOD [https://www.crediblecatholic.com/pdf/7E-P2/7E-BB1.pdf#P1V1]

Some question why God, if He exists, insists on being so hidden; others wonder at how He could be so evident yet remain unseen. [7, 8, 9]

Consider that playing 'hide and seek' requires both 'hiding' and 'seeking' in order for the game to make sense. Also, consider from our experience that relationships having an element of mystery bring enhanced interest, depth, and desire. Perhaps an indirect relationship of subtle mystery poses an appealing alternative to one that might be otherwise overwhelming and imposing – maybe even intimidating - in the harsh and direct light of stark, immense reality.

The ability to freely choose participation in relationship - or not - is most fundamental to its authenticity and legitimacy. It is the difference between conquest and respectful engagement of the other - reaching out, inviting and drawing toward oneself in love, beauty, goodness, and truth.

1.3   We are Uniquely Created
We are uniquely created as human beings in image and likeness of Him.

1.3.1   We are of spirit.

1.3.2   We are embodied in matter.

1.3.3   We are time-bound in this life, but have an eternal destiny.

1.3.4   We are endowed with intellect for knowing what is true.

1.3.5   We are endowed with free will for choosing what is good.

1.3.6   We are invited into relationship with Him in love as children and Father.

The degree to which we are uniquely made is almost unfathomable.

The complexity and uniqueness of our physical DNA connects us with, yet distinctly separates us from, every other human being who has ever existed. We are each literally one-of-a-kind; both a product of our lineage and the direct offspring of our parents. We did not exist prior to our moment of conception – a moment in which the universe was quite literally and irreversibly changed by our presence – but we will exist forever after, [10] for all eternity. [11]

While we are finite creatures of body and soul [12] with limited capabilities and attributes, it could be said that in a sense, we contain an infinity within us – not only in our physical make-up, but also in dimensions of our giftings, temperaments, and personalities which in turn extend into the myriad actions and initiatives flowing out from them over the course of our lives. [13, 14]

---

[7] "...science as the study of the handiwork of God" (p. 28) Ref 8.2 Trasancos, S. A. (2016). Particles of Faith.

[8] Ref 8.2.1 Dr. Stacy Trasanick for (Steubenville Conferences). (2019, 9 27). Dr. Stacy Trasancos - The Faith and Science Conflict Myth (2019 Defending the Faith Conference). Retrieved from YouTube – excerpt (39:07 – 45:30), "Chemistry Glasses": https://www.youtube.com/embed/upAjw3YO7n4?start=2347&end=2730

[9] Ref 5.9 Therrien, M. (2020). The Catholic Faith Explained – "4. How God Reveals Himself"

[10] ...which follows if the premises and conclusions of this text are found reasonable....

[11] Ref 8.13 Chris Stefanick (for Real Life Catholic). (2014, 9 30). You're Kind of a Big Deal. Retrieved from YouTube: [https://www.youtube.com/watch?v=d_34gjdHp3M]

[12] Ref 5.13 Spitzer, F. R. (2017). Big Book - Credible Catholic. [https://www.crediblecatholic.com/big-book] - Volume 2 – EVIDENCE OF OUR TRANSPHYSICAL SOUL: [https://www.crediblecatholic.com/pdf/7E-P1/7E-BB2.pdf#P1V2]

[13] Refs 12.1, 12.2 Gallup's StrengthsFinder assessment utilizes 34 signature themes to characterize and rank particular capabilities; they indicate the probability of meeting somebody with the same top 5 in the same order as being 1 in 33 million. By extension, the probability of meeting another person with all 34 in exactly the same sequence would be astronomical. Adding in the other personal dimensions makes the uniqueness all the more profound.

[14] Ref 8.16 Ortberg, J. (2005). God is Closer Than You Think – "Spiritual Pathways"; describes seven different 'pathways' through which individuals seek relationship with God according to aspects of their personality (e.g., intellectual, relational, serving...)

2   The Problem

We are at risk of eternal separation from Him.

2.1   We Were Connected
We were cared for and related to as children of a loving father from the beginning. [15]

2.1.1   We were originally created in perfect relationship with Him.

2.1.2   He loves all of us and each of us.

2.1.3   He is writing a story in collaboration with us.

2.1.4   He is desiring of our genuine loving response and participation.

2.1.5   He gives boundaries for our care and rightly ordered relationship with him.

2.1.6   He is capable of controlling, but respects our choosing.

2.1.7   We are free to turn toward and be a part with, to express love in collaboration.

2.1.8   We are free to turn away and be apart from, to withhold love in opposition.

2.1.9   We are free to express our own view of meaning & determine our destiny by our choices.

He is writing a story of existence and being, with and through all of His creation. We are part of it, and are invited to co-author as it unfolds in time. It is by nature not a prescribed and scripted presentation, but an expressive, spontaneous, and inspired collaboration.

2.2   We Broke Away
We damaged the perfect relationship in our pridefulness. [16, 17]

2.2.1   Our original ancestors were deceived by influence contrary to Him.

2.2.2   They acted in opposition to the right order of relationship.

2.2.3   Disorder, sin, sickness, and death were introduced into material creation.

2.2.4   Defect, blemish, stain, and corruption were introduced into spiritual creation.

2.2.5   Legacy effects remain through the ages, still evidenced in the world and in our souls.

---

[15] Ref 5.5 Hahn, S. (1998). A Father Who Keeps His Promises: God's Covenant Love in Scripture.
[16] Ref 5.9 Therrien, M. (2020). The Catholic Faith Explained – "10. The Story of Adam and Eve"
[17] (Ibid) "12. The Fall from Grace and the Need for Redemption"

Our lived experience and our current world of existence bears witness to the blessed yet, in many ways, unfortunate state of human affairs. There is a brokenness, a fallenness, a certain state of disorder evident in a general sense that, although there is much beauty and goodness to behold, things are not entirely as they should be given the significant degree of ugliness and suffering which remains. [18]

So, it is now, and has been throughout history since the time of our original ancestors. And though we did not participate directly in their actions against right order and relationship, we all carry within ourselves remnants of this spiritual disconnect. Much like we inherit attributes within our physical DNA, we can think of this in terms of residual defects inherited in the 'spiritual DNA' of our souls.

2.3   We Are Lost on Our Own

We remain separated from Him by virtue of our own choosing, not by His turning from us or condemnation.

2.3.1   We can be eternally separated from Him if relationship is not repaired and maintained.

2.3.2   We are not capable, on our own, of repairing this relationship once broken.

2.3.3   We need to accept the repair and maintain relationship in this life to carry it into eternity.

Should we choose to live out of this brokenness, and fail to be healed and return to right relationship, we will live in eternal separation from Him and His love. We know this from His revelation in history and through what He taught and lived as described in the section which follows.   From this context and in relation to our earlier question of whether it is "reasonable to believe", it is relevant to further consider, "what is risked, what is to be gained, and what stands to be lost in believing or not?".

---

[18] Ref 5.13 Spitzer, F. R. (2017). Big Book - Credible Catholic [https://www.crediblecatholic.com/big-book/] - Volume 14 – SUFFERING, SPIRITUAL EVIL, AND JESUS' DEFEAT OF SATAN [https://www.crediblecatholic.com/pdf/P14/BB14.pdf#P1V14]

3   The Solution

"The days are coming, says the Lord,
when I will make a new covenant with the house of Israel and the house of Judah".
— Jeremiah 31:31

"For the Son of God became man so that we might become God."
— St. Athanasius [19, 20]

3.1   He Reached Out to Us
God, in His infinite love and mercy, sought to repair this broken relationship through a series of covenants.

3.1.1   Salvation History is our lived experience of God offering a series of relational covenants.

3.1.2   Each covenant represented a deeper, broader encounter in relationship and commitment.

3.1.3   We engaged in these covenants imperfectly, waxing and waning.

3.1.4   Each covenant, in some way broken on our part, pointed toward an ultimate fulfillment.

In the history of the ancient Hebrew people, [21] a series of covenantal relationships are recognized which centered on their interactions with God through specific leaders having increasing spheres of authority (Adam, Noah, Abram – later known as Abraham, Moses, and David). [22, 23]

In some ways you could almost imagine after all of preceding history, with mankind's alternating periods of closeness to Him and falling away, that He finally threw up His hands and said "I'm just going to have to come down there and show you myself!".

---

[19] Ref 1.3 CCC 460; not in a total and complete sense, but in finite likeness. See also Ref 5.12.

[20] Ref 5.12 Beaumont, Douglas M. (for Catholic Answers). (2019, 9 23). Can Man Become God? Retrieved from Catholic Answers: [https://www.catholic.com/magazine/online-edition/can-man-become-god]

[21] Ref 4.2 Schoeman, R. H. (2003). Salvation of From the Jews: The Role of Judaism in Salvation History...

[22] Ref 2.5 Cavins, J., Gray, T., & Christmyer, S. (2003 (revised 10/04)). Bible Timeline Chart.

[23] Ref 5.5 Hahn, S. (1998). A Father Who Keeps His Promises: God's Covenant Love in Scripture.

3.2 He Came for Us

"I have come into the world as light,
so that whoever believes in me may not remain in darkness.
If anyone hears my words and does not keep them, I do not judge him;
for I did not come to judge the world but to save the world."
John 12:46-47

"...For this purpose I was born and for this purpose I have come into the world - to
bear witness to the truth. Everyone who is of the truth listens to my voice."
John 18:37

"...the truth will set you free."
John 8:32

God himself enters into His own creation, taking on flesh as a man – the 'God-Man'. [24, 25, 26, 27, 28, 29]

3.2.1   He was conceived of a woman supernaturally.

3.2.2   He is one person having two natures (fully divine, fully human).

3.2.3   He grew to manhood and at the age of thirty began public ministry.

3.2.4   He taught with wisdom and authority.

3.2.5   He performed healings and other miracles.

3.2.6   He fulfilled many prophesies.

3.2.7   He claimed to be the 'Son of God', one with 'God the Father'.

3.2.8   He was accused of blasphemy and opposition to imperial rule, and was put to death.

3.2.9   He rose from the dead on the third day following his death and burial.

At a specific time and place, the Creator condescends to quite literally enter into His own creation as a human being – Jesus the Christ (i.e., "the anointed one"), the perfect and complete instantiation of union between divinity and humanity – born of a woman, conceived by the Holy Spirit. [30]

The person of Jesus remains most pivotal in the history of mankind; so much so, that we divide our measure of time in terms of 'BC' and 'AD' with the transition point being the occasion of His birth.

His existence as a historical figure is essentially undisputed among scholars. His reputation as a wise and learned teacher, theologian, and philosopher is widely recognized. His identity as the long-awaited and foretold Messiah [31] for the ancient Hebrew people is disputed. His nature and being as the 'Son of God' - literally, God incarnate - remains the most provocative and consequential consideration posed throughout all of human history. [32]

---

[24] Resource 1)a) "Someone has Come to Fight", Fr. John Riccardo, Acts XXIX [https://www.youtube.com/watch?v=XqafKxFiktQ]

[25] Ref 3.1 Pitre, B. (2016). The Case for Jesus: The Biblical and Historical Evidence for Christ.

[26] Ref 2.1 D'Ambrosio, M., Cavins, J., & Sri, E. (2020). The Jesus Timeline Chart.

[27] Ref 3.2 Strobel, L. (1998 (ePub format)). The Case for Christ.

[28] Outline elements & CCC refs derived from Ref 5.8 Lukefahr, Fr Oscar (2nd 1995). "We Believe..." - A Survey... pages 23-33

[29] Ref 5.9 Therrien, M. (2020). The Catholic Faith Explained – "14. Jesus the Messiah"

[30] Ref 1.3 CCC 484 - 534

[31] Ref 3.3 McDowell, J. (1972, 1979). Evidence that Demands a Verdict - Volume 1, pages 173-176 - Over 300 distinct predictions of the Old Testament are fulfilled in Jesus, including elements of his birth, death, and resurrection. The probability of all these together being fulfilled so distinctly and definitively in the life of a single person are astronomical.

[32] Ref 1.3 CCC 535 - 542, 551 - 553

7

Those who recognize as valid His claims to divinity likewise acknowledge that His life, death, and resurrection reconciled mankind to God once-and-for-all through a perfect sacrifice and served to show us through perfect example how to live in loving relationship with God and with others.

His claims to divinity [33] were accompanied by supernatural occurrences – healings and other miracles, including resurrection of persons deceased – which convinced many of their authenticity. [34, 35] As further evidence for validity of His claims, others point as well to the continuing spread of His message and persistence of the Church He founded throughout the centuries up to the present moment, despite significant periods of opposition and persecution.

And all this, emerging from the context of very humble beginnings as a poor child born in a manger to a seemingly insignificant family. His childhood, adolescence, and young adulthood were spent in relative obscurity (despite a particular noteworthy occurrence in which He was found teaching in the Temple in Jerusalem at the age of twelve). [36]

His public ministry was both foretold and initiated by the enigmatic figure of John the Baptist – marked by a supernatural occurrence at the time of His baptism in the Jordan river [37] and followed by a 40-day period of prayer and fasting spent in the wilderness. His inner circle of twelve were then assembled and accompanied Him through the next three years spent in the public eye.

His reception by the main groupings of society in His day (Sadducees – common citizens; Zealots – revolutionaries; Pharisees – fundamentalist religious leaders; and Essenes – desert spiritualists) was influenced by each of their respective viewpoints. In all cases, they failed to fully appreciate and accept His revealed identity as Son of God, largely because He did not fit any of their varying preconceived notions of the foretold Messiah. Regardless of their acceptance or rejection, He consistently resisted attempts to proclaim him king of an earthly kingdom and continued to call them to repentance from their worldly and sinful ways.

The conspiracy and intrigue leading to His eventual arrest, persecution, and death was orchestrated among detractors with plot and drama rivalling the best of current day suspense novels. And all the while, He humbly submitted to events as they unfolded despite a presumed capability to oppose and alter them. [38, 39]

Why the crucifixion - for what purpose? [40, 41] Theologically, it is understood to have been the means by which we are freed from the bonds of sin and redeemed [42] thus reconciling us to God, overcoming the separation between us due to sin, and reestablishing our broken relationship. In its essence, it shows us what perfect love looks like. [43]

His crucifixion was followed by a hasty burial before Sabbath and was done, uncharacteristically, without anointing of the body. This circumstance led to the dramatic discovery two days later when women returned to anoint him in the tomb, only to find His body is missing – the stone of the tomb rolled back, the seal broken, tomb empty. Only His burial shroud remained [44], signifying what they would come to realize as His resurrection [45, 46] when He later began appearing in their midst on various occasions.

---

[33] Ref 8.1 Cronin, F. (2020). *The World According to God*; Chapters on Jesus in History

[34] Ref 1.3 CCC 547 - 549

[35] Ref 3.3 McDowell, J. (1972, 1979). Evidence that Demands a Verdict - Volume 1, page 122-123: Occurrences in the natural realm, physical healings, resurrections of the dead, and power over demonic influences are all cited. Miracles are manifestations of God's presence and grace; revelations of His love, mercy, and grace; free actions of His sovereign will. Those performed by Jesus were sometimes due to faith and sometimes not, but always resulted in an increase of faith for those involved.

[36] See Ref 9.2. The Rosary is a devotional prayer in which the life of Christ is meditated upon. There are a total of 20 specific events which are grouped into four sets of ten 'mysteries associated with periods in His life (birth/early childhood, public ministry, passion/death, resurrection). The devotion is most fully expressed in the form of a 'Scriptural Rosary' in which a verse of scripture is associated with each of the events.

[37] "And a voice came from heaven, "You are my beloved Son;4 with you I am well pleased." Mark 1:11

[38] Ref 1.3 CCC 554 - 594

[39] Ref 1.3 CCC 595 - 598

[40] Ref 1.3 CCC 599 - 623

[41] Ref 8.15 Gumbel, N. (1993, 1996, 2003, 2010, 2016). Questions of Life. (eBook), page 43: We are "justified" (Rom 5:1-11)...imagine a judge who in justice, assigns a penalty and then, in love, pays the cost for a friend who comes before him in court.

[42] Ref 1.1 ESV Rom 5:1-11

[43] Ref 1.1 ESV John 14:6, John 15:13

[44] Ref 5.13 Spitzer, F. R. (2017). *Big Book* - Credible Catholic [https://www.crediblecatholic.com/big-book/] - Volume 3 – EVIDENCE FOR THE HISTORICITY AND DIVINITY OF JESUS CHRIST, Chapter Eight - Science and **The Shroud of Turin** [https://www.crediblecatholic.com/pdf/7E-P4/7E-BB3.pdf#P1V3C8]

3.3   He Left Us Means and a Mission

"All power in heaven and on earth has been given to me.
Go, therefore, and make disciples of all nations,
baptizing them in the name of the Father, and of the son, and of the Holy Spirit,
teaching them to observe all that I have commanded you.
And behold, I am with you always, until the end of the age"
—— *Matthew 26:18-20*

He left us a Church to lead and guide us over time, to give us the sacramental means to enter into relationship with Him and with each other, and to provide us the capability to repair brokenness which enters into our lives due to continuing shortcomings and imperfections. [47]

3.3.1   He appeared to many witnesses for forty days following His resurrection.

3.3.2   He offered the glorious gift of eternal life together with Him and God the Father.

3.3.3   He described the dim alternative of eternal life separated from Him and God the Father.

3.3.4   He founded a Church as a means for us to be healed and reconciled to Him and to all.

3.3.5   He promised to return at the end of time.

3.3.6   He promised to send us His Spirit for guidance and support in the interim.

3.3.7   He authorized & sent His followers to teach, heal, minister, and call others in His name.

3.3.8   He promised to be with them until the end of time.

3.3.9   He ascended and disappeared into the sky.

He calls us to holiness and perfection that will be ultimately fulfilled upon our entrance into Heaven on our departing from this world. Our body and spirit, which are temporarily separated at death, will be reunited and glorified, and we will share eternal life with Him.

The Church that He founded [48] guides us on the journey through life and into eternity. Its nature is reflected in the names given it throughout sacred texts – the "Body of Christ" [49], the "Bride of Christ" [50] – with its mission being to serve as the connection between God and mankind, and to do so with the person of Christ as the focal point. [51] Its essential purpose and that of its members can be stated most simply: "To bring Christ to the world, and bring the world to Christ". In and through this Church, He provides the means by which our spiritual brokenness can be healed and we can return to wholeness in right relationship with Him and with others. [52, 53]

---

[45] Ref 1.1 ESV Matt 28, Mark 16, Luke 24, John 20,21

[46] Ref 3.4 Habermas, G. (2012, 11 8). *The Resurrection Argument That Changed a Generation of Scholars - Gary Habermas at UCSB*. Retrieved from YouTube: [https://www.youtube.com/watch?v=ay_Db4RwZ_M]

[47] Resource 2)b) ECHO 11 - 4 Marks of the Church [https://vimeo.com/192369178]

[48] Ref 1.3 CCC 748 - 812

[49] Ref 1.1 ESV Col 1:18

[50] Ref 1.1 ESV Eph 5:25-27

[51] "The Chosen" is a widely acclaimed and engaging depiction of who the Apostles were and dramatized accounts of their calling by Jesus. The Series and Background: [https://watch.angelstudios.com/thechosen],
Season 1: [https://watch.angelstudios.com/thechosen/watch?vid=S1],
Season 2: available at same link via pull-down tab

[52] Ref 5.11 Kaczor, Christopher (for Catholic Answers). (2007). Seven Principals of Catholic Social Teaching. [https://www.catholic.com/magazine/print-edition/seven-principles-of-catholic-social-teaching]

[53] Ref 7.11 Compendium of the Social Doctrine of the Church, Pontifical Council for Justice and Peace (2004, 4 2): [http://www.vatican.va/roman_curia/pontifical_councils/justpeace/documents/rc_pc_justpeace_doc_20060526_compendio-dott-soc_en.html]

It is 'one' [54], meaning, a single institution as Christ was a single individual, founded upon one leader – Peter – to carry it forward in His love and with His authority [55]. As Christ was made visible in the flesh, the Church is made visible in its common profession of faith, common celebration of sacraments, and the current living successors to His first followers, the Apostles, [56, 57] together with all of the faithful.

While it has been fragmented by divisions over time, its original grounding is yet passed on in a thread of continuity and in its fullness within the Catholic Church. All separated portions remain in connection and relationship to varying degrees according to their faithfulness to Christ.

It is 'holy',[58] a divine institution created by the Father, established by the Son, guided and animated by the Holy Spirit - bound to Him in a spousal relationship as 'Bride of Christ' whom He loved and "gave himself up for, that he might sanctify her..." [59]. So, while made and maintained holy in this manner to be the Kingdom of God manifest on Earth, it remains not yet perfected this side of eternity with its membership consisting of flawed human beings – treasure held in "earthen vessels" [60]; a mix of growth comprised of both "weeds and wheat" [61].

It is 'universal' [62] (i.e., Catholic, deriving from the Greek *katholikos*) in its representation of the fullness of the deposit of faith (in whole, total), and in its applicability and availability to all people.

It is 'apostolic' [63] as is built on the foundation and authorization of Christ [64] through His initial followers, the Apostles [65, 66], and has been carried to the present day by succession through the ritual 'laying of hands' [67] in a chain of formal ordination that can be traced down through the centuries.

In a quite literal sense, attending and participating fully in the particular form of worship generally referred to as "the Mass" (see 6.1.4, *Engaging worship – The Mass and The Sacraments*) on any given Sunday confirms one as belonging to an ancient 2000+ year-old Christian tradition having a 4000+ year-old preceding lineage of belief commonly shared with other 'Abrahamic' faiths.[68]

---

[54] Ref 1.3 CCC 813 - 822
[55] Ref 1.1 ESV Matt 16:18, Col 3:14
[56] Media 8)i) *Saint Paul, Apostle to the Gentiles* from "Lives of Saints", Published by John J. Crawley & Co., Inc. - excerpt via EWTN website: [https://www.ewtn.com/catholicism/library/saint-paul-apostle-to-the-gentiles-5731]
[57] Media 8)j) *Saint Peter, Prince of the Apostles* from "Lives of Saints", Published by John J. Crawley & Co., Inc. - excerpt via EWTN website: [https://www.ewtn.com/catholicism/library/saint-peter-prince-of-the-apostles-5749]
[58] Ref 1.3 CCC 823 - 829
[59] Ref 1.1 ESV Eph 5:25-27
[60] Ref 1.1 ESV 2 Cor 4:7
[61] Ref 1.1 ESV Matt 13:24-43
[62] Ref 1.3 CCC 830 - 856
[63] Ref 1.3 CCC 857 - 865
[64] Ref 1.1 ESV Matt 28:18-20
[65] Ref 1.1 ESV Eph 2:19-22
[66] Ref 1.1 ESV 2 Cor 3, 2 Cor 5, 2 Cor 6, 1 Cor 4
[67] Ref 1.1 ESV Acts 6:6. Acts 13:3. 2 Tim 1:6
[68] Ref 1.3 CCC 839 - 841

4   The Legacy

"...beauty ever ancient and ever new."
St. Augustine, Confessions – Book X

4.1   The Message (What did He teach?)

"The time is fulfilled, and the kingdom of God is at hand;
repent and believe in the gospel."
— Mark 1:15

4.1.1   Summary of His Teachings – Love God, Love Your Neighbor as Yourself

If one were to summarize the essence of Jesus's teachings as outlined in the four books of the Bible [69] which contain them (i.e., the "Gospel" narratives – Matthew, Mark, Luke, and John [70]), it might look something like Figure 4-1. All of the passages which involve Him speaking (often printed in 'red letters' for easy emphasis) could be readily associated with one or more of the blocks shown.

Everything He is and does represents what it means to be in right relationship with God, and He explicitly identifies this relationship as one of 'child to Father' (a scandalous and misunderstood claim at the time, which remains so yet today for some). It is therefore most fundamentally one grounded in love. He lays out the means for engaging and growing in this relationship, extends it to include right relationship with others, and shows the way in which God intends that all be drawn into it - both now in this life, and in a promised eternal life after death.

The process of growing to be like Jesus has two components: 1) receiving and cooperating with His supernatural grace and the influence of the Holy Spirit, and 2) putting forth effort to engage in prayer and study of scripture (more on this in later sections).

Figure 4-1 shows the process as a sort of 'loop' beginning with and returning to God - an iterative process, since in our imperfect human nature, we grow progressively in increments over time towards 'perfection' in likeness to Jesus while continuing to engage in these two areas.

It presents an interesting thought experiment to imagine what the world and this life would be like if every person on the planet sought to foster such a relationship with God and with each other. Alternatively, one could imagine what it would be like if every person operated in a manner *opposed* to the principal characteristics of such relationship. It is fair to say that we all see and even experience examples of both of these nearly every day. [71]

---

[69] "The Bible" being the informal name given to definitive collection of books which formally comprise Sacred Scripture (see 4.2.5.2)

[70] Ref 6.7 The National Catholic Education Commission (NCEC), Australian Catholic Bishops Conference. (n.d.). The Gospels. Retrieved from Scripture for Teachers: [https://scripture.catholic.edu.au/index.php/home/foundations/the-gospels/]

[71] Ref 2)a) ANIMA – a three-part production on the life of faith (Crux, Kenosis, Blaze) [

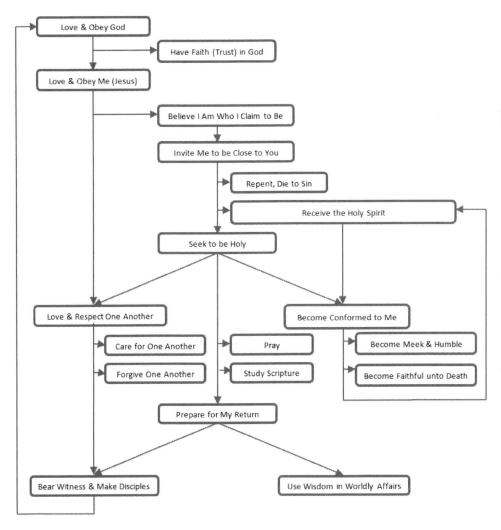

Figure 4-1 What did He teach?

4.1.2   Highlights of His Teachings – Parables, Exhortations, Revelations

He taught in colorful stories called parables [72, 73, 74] having particular, consistent themes, e.g.:

1) The kingdom of God is present in Jesus, like a hidden treasure, a pearl.
2) The Gospel (the "Good News"), is that God wants to give mercy and forgiveness to all.
3) We cannot receive God's mercy unless we share it with others. (The Good Samaritan)
4) God is almighty, and the kingdom that God establishes through Jesus cannot be destroyed.
5) All this calls for a response. We must change our lives and put God's kingdom first.

He called his followers and listeners, exhorting them to a counter-cultural way of life which 'raised the bar' relative to prior moral perspectives. This is classically evident in perhaps His most famous and comprehensive teaching, The Sermon on the Mount [75] which included:

1) The Beatitudes
2) Moral demands; fidelity to God's law, victory over anger and lust, commitment in marriage, forgiveness, love of enemies, generosity.
3) How to pray, with the "Our Father" prayer as prime example. [76]
4) God first, second to nothing else (money, etc. - power, prestige, pleasure, possessions...) [77]
5) A pattern for living that is psychologically and spiritually sound: healthy self-esteem, generous love for others, belief in God as the origin and goal in life.

He revealed aspects of God that could not otherwise have been known through human experience and reason alone, and pointed to the ultimate path and goal for all of us. A concise summary example is The Last Supper Discourse [78]:

1) Reveals the Trinity.
2) Commands to love one another as he has loved us.
3) Promises a peace that cannot be taken away.
4) Not even death can separate us from the life, love, joy, and peace He came to bring.

In summary, He clearly sought to convey the understanding that faith in God is the most central consideration from which a fulfilling and fruitful life is lived, not a minor or peripheral concern.

---

[72] Ref 1.3 CCC 543-546
[73] Ref 6.5 The National Catholic Education Commission (NCEC), Australian Catholic Bishops Conference. (n.d.). What is a Parable? Retrieved from Scripture for Teachers: [https://scripture.catholic.edu.au/index.php/home/foundations/what-is-a-parable/]
[74] Ref 6.5 Archdiocese of Brisbane, Australia. (2019, 8 12). The Parable Podcasts, YouTube Playlist (7 Episodes). Retrieved from Episodes 1: Intro; 2: Prodigal Son; 3: Good Samaritan; 4: Rich Man & Lazarus; 5: Labourers in the Vineyard; 6: The Talents; 7: Great Banquet: [https://www.youtube.com/watch?v=LiEc-Z-J67E&list=PL8-1Dil2Zzb_2SbupaDKZTjyfsY32V7UY]
[75] Ref 1.3 CCC 543-544, 1716 - 1729
[76] Appendix - Prayers : "The Lord's Prayer – the model prayer"
[77] Ref 8.11 Joseph, M. (2018). Overwhelming Pursuit: Stop Chasing Your Life and Live.
[78] Ref 1.3 CCC 2604, 2746 - 2751

4.2   The Medium (Knowing *about* Him)

"Faith seeking understanding" — St Anselm

4.2.1   His legacy of interaction with mankind was compiled and conveyed over millennia.

4.2.2   His legacy was compiled and conveyed initially through oral, and later written means.

4.2.3   His legacy has preserved integrity & coherence via authoritative oversight & guidance.

4.2.4   His legacy has stability which rests upon three supporting elements.

4.2.5   The Church He founded has responsibility and authority to faithfully convey this legacy.

God speaks to us here and now through prayer, but He also speaks through the legacy of His interaction with mankind in history. This legacy, [79] sometimes referred to as the "deposit of faith", is composed of three basic, complimentary, inter-related, and inter-dependent elements. [80, 81] They can be thought of and illustrated in simple terms as 'three legs of a stool' on which faith rests and is passed on (see Figure 4-2):

1) Sacred Tradition > The "Spoken Word", the lived faith in Church teachings and practices
2) Sacred Scripture > The "Written Word", the Bible [82]
3) The Magisterium > The Word made Flesh, the life and teachings of Christ in 1) & 2) above,
    carried forward in the Teaching Authority granted by Him
    to the Apostles and their living successors

Figure 4-2 The Deposit of Faith ("3-Legged Stool")

---

[79] Apostolates 27)a) Hunt, D. A. (2014, 3 22). Charlotte Catholic Men's Conference 2014 - Dr. Allen Hunt. Retrieved from YouTube - Dan Trapini: https://www.youtube.com/watch?v=S8OYTFKrH40

[80] Ref 6.3 The National Catholic Education Commission (NCEC), Australian Catholic Bishops Conference. (n.d.). Catholic Teaching on Sacred Scripture. Retrieved from Scripture for Teachers: [https://scripture.catholic.edu.au/index.php/home/foundations/catholic-teaching-on-sacred-scripture/]

[81] Ref 1.3 CCC 95

[82] Ref 1.3 CCC 101 - 141

4.2.5.1   Sacred Tradition

Sacred Tradition, the "oral" component of the 'Deposit of Faith', is the stream of mankind's lived experience and interactions with God which flows continuously throughout human history down to the present day from its origins extending even into pre-history.

It is the context in which Sacred Scripture was compiled, and it eventually transitioned from solely oral transmission into being assembled and passed on in documents describing the cumulative and developing understanding of faith in God as lived and experienced. While considered to be authoritative (having been authored by authoritative sources i.e., by those having Teaching Authority – see 4.2.5.3 – or those designated/approved by such), these documents are of solely human authorship and remain distinct from Sacred Scripture, which is particularly and uniquely understood to have been divinely inspired.

In total, this written form of the "oral" tradition includes documents such as the cumulative writing of the early Church leadership (referred to as the 'Early Church Fathers', or 'Patriarchs'), writings and sermons of Saints, approved writings of theologians and scholars, official Church documents or proclamations (e.g., apostolic exhortations, encyclicals, decrees, dogmatic constitutions, etc.), and proceedings from official Church Councils (meetings of leadership). It can be useful to think this collection as sort of a 'Christian family journal' which tells our family story of lived experience in the faith, and provides a context for interpreting its meaning, influence, and relevance.

Perhaps most significantly, there have also been periodic issuances of integrated documents for use in teaching and formation (referred to as 'catechisms', originating from the Greek for 'instruct by word of mouth' [83]). Such 'catechisms' can be thought of as reference summary guides to all other the varied sources. They have been compiled at various points in time, the most recent of which is simply titled the *"Catechism of the Catholic Church"*. [84] It is organized into four parts (the "Four Pillars": Creed, Worship, Moral Life, and Prayer) which address the basic areas relevant to understanding and living the faith, and which have served historically as a consistent organizing structure for describing the faith. It has extensive indexing, cross-referencing, and footnotes to scripture and reference documents for deep study, and also has short 'In Brief' bulletized outlines at the end of each section to allow for more casual reading, familiarity, review, and quick reference. It is the ultimate "go-to" resource to check on "what the Church teaches" relative to any question that arises, and provides insights into not only 'what' is believed, but 'why' it is believed.

Alternate supplementary forms or descriptions of the catechism been developed for brevity [85, 86] or packaged for specific regional/culture context. [87]

4.2.5.2   Sacred Scripture [88]

""Statistically speaking, the Gospels are the greatest literature ever written.
They are read by more people, quoted by more authors, translated into more
tongues, represented in more art, set to more music, than any other book or books
written by any man in any century in any land. But the words of Christ are not great
on the grounds that they have such a statistical edge over anybody else's words.
They are read more, quoted more, loved more, believed more, and translated more
because they are the greatest words ever spoken.
And where is their greatness?
Their greatness lies in the pure, lucid spirituality in dealing clearly, definitively, and
authoritatively with the greatest problems that throb in the human breast; namely,

---

[83] [https://www.etymonline.com/word/catechism]
[84] Ref 1.3 CCC - Catholic Church. (2016). *Catechism of the Catholic Church* (2nd ed.).
    [online via https://www.vatican.va/archive/ENG0015/_INDEX.HTM]
[85] Ref 5.6, USCCB. (2005). Compendium of the Catechism of the Catholic Church.
[86] Ref 5.8 Lukefahr, F. O. (1990, 2nd Edition 1995). "We Believe..." - A Survey of the Catholic Faith, 2nd Edition.
[87] Ref 1.3 USCCB. (2004, November). United States Catholic Catechism for Adults.
    [online via: https://www.usccb.org/beliefs-and-teachings/what-we-believe/catechism/us-catholic-catechism-for-adults]
[88] Ref 6.2 Akin, J. (2019). *The Bible is a Catholic Book*

> *Who is God? Does He love Me? What should I do to please Him? How does He look at my sin? How can I be forgiven? Where will I go when I die? How must I treat others?*
>
> *No other man's words have the appeal of Jesus' words because no other man can answer these fundamental human questions as Jesus answered them. They are the kind of words and the kind of answers we would expect God to give, and we who believe in Jesus' deity have no problem as to why these words came from His mouth."*
>
> — *Bernard Ramm:* [89]

Sacred Scripture, the "written" component of the 'Deposit of Faith', is commonly referred to as "The Bible". It is actually a collection of books held by believers to be the divinely inspired 'Word of God', that is, the text was written by human authors who were guided by the Holy Spirit – not in a manner of direct dictation, but in their own language and style with content having been imparted through divine influence.

It is comprised of two major groups of books:

1) Old Testament: corresponding to the Old covenant(s) between God & ancient Hebrews [46 books]
   From Creation to 100 years before Christ, covering Salvation History, i.e., the interactions between God and the ancient Hebrews, while pointing to the coming Messiah.

   a. Pentateuch: (5) [Genesis, Exodus, Leviticus, Numbers, Deuteronomy]
      First 5 books; Mosaic Law---Story of God's liberation of the Hebrew people.
      Meant to answer the basic questions in life and explain origins of the Jewish people.
      Written 1000 to 550 BC, edited 550 to 400 BC

   b. Historical books: (16) [Joshua, Judges, 1-2 Samuel, 1-2 Kings, 1-2 Chronicles, Ezra, Nehemiah, 1-2 Maccabees]
      [(Special) Ruth, Tobit, Judith, Esther]
      Entry of Israelites into Promised Land. Covers from 1210 BC to Maccabean wars 142 BC.
      Primary purpose to teach the story of the encounter between God and humankind.

   c. Prophets: (18) [(Major) Isaiah, Jeremiah, Ezekiel, Daniel, Lamentations, Baruch]
      [(Minor) Hosea, Amos, Micah, Nahum, Habakkuk, Zephaniah, Haggai, Zechariah, Obadiah, Joel, Jonah, Malachi]
      A prophet is one who "speaks for God" with a focus on the need to draw back to God's love.
      Whenever God's people were unfaithful, He inspires a reforming, counter-movement via the prophets.

   d. Wisdom: (7) Job, Psalms, Proverbs, Ecclesiastes, Song of Songs, Wisdom, Sirach
      Poetry, wise sayings, prayers, love songs.
      Wisdom writers portray a successful response to life in God's world.

2) New Testament: corresponding to the New covenant between God & all Mankind [27 books]
   From the time of Christ's birth, through emergence of the early church, and speaking onward to all of mankind, while pointing to the returning Messiah at the end of time, beginning eternity.

   a. Gospels: (4) Matthew, Mark, Luke, John
      Story of Jesus' life and ministry. Considered heart of all scriptures. Mark written first.

---

[89] Ref 3.3, McDowell, J. (1972, 1979). Evidence that Demands a Verdict - Volume 1, ebook (Kindle Edition), page 129

b. Acts of the Apostles: (1) Acts
Some consider this the 2nd volume of Luke's Gospel. Early days of Christian community.

c. Letters (Epistles): (21) [(Pauline) 1-2 Thessalonians, Galatians, 1-2 Corinthians, Romans, Philippians, Colossians, Ephesians, Philemon, 102 Timothy, Titus] [(Other) 1-2-3 John, 1-2 Peter, James, Jude, Hebrews]
St. Paul's letters to different Christian communities. Others are various authors writing on significant topics important for the whole (catholic) church.

d. Revelation: (1) Revelation
"Apocalypse" literature which uses figurative language, symbols and numbers, visions, heavenly messengers, and picturesque descriptions of the struggle between good and evil.
A symbolic book that concerns Christianity's final conquest during the last days.

It is said that the Old Testament is revealed in the New, and the New Testament is concealed in the Old. Transition between them is marked by the figure of Jesus, who is said to transform and fulfill the Old in the New. [90]
Many discover that one of the most surprising and challenging things about first engaging the Bible is the arrangement of the books; they are not placed – front to back, i.e., cover to cover - in historical-chronological order according to subject matter. Although, as we shall see, scripture is not solely or even most importantly a recording of history (though for many books, there are certainly significant historical components) this simple - but not obvious – fact can be the single most enlightening (or confusing) key (or impediment) to making sense of the over-arching storyline. A number of resources have been compiled to specifically address this most fundamental concern. [91, 92, 93]
Reading and interpreting the Bible requires attention to the various literary forms employed for the books, e.g., hymns, prayers, poems, stories, historical narratives, prophecies, exhortations, letters, biographical accounts. Much like any modern author, the writers chose literary forms for their texts according to their purpose and means by which they could best tell others of an experience. Each literary form must be read and interpreted accordingly, much the same as one would read and interpret a newspaper editorial differently than front-page news, or a movie review in the style section, or a segment of the sports page – context is key.
Also, one must consider variations in the sense of scripture, determining the style and context in order to determine the degree to which the text should be handled literally, or perhaps symbolically or metaphorically. These distinctions for interpretation take place within the Tradition and Teaching Authority in the Church, assisted by clergy, scholars, and theologians.
Much guidance has been made available to support individual prayer with scripture and biblical study. [94, 95, 96, 97]
At base, the guiding principle is for scripture passages to be interpreted in the context of 'divine revelation', that is to say, within the whole of Sacred Scripture, Sacred Tradition, and according to what is known as the 'analogy of faith' – a term referring to the harmony and coherence of the individual components when taken together as a whole. [98, 99]

---

[90] Ref 1.3 CCC 129, St Augustine
[91] Ref 2.5 2.5. Cavins, J., Gray, T., & Christmyer, S. (2003 (revised 10/04)). Bible Timeline Chart [https://ascensionpress.com/products/great-adventure-bible-timeline-chart?variant=31113215279140]
[92] Resource 4)a) Great Adventure Bible Study [https://ascensionpress.com/pages/the-great-adventure]
[93] Resources 4)b) and 4)c) Fr. Mike Schmitz, Bible in a Year podcast, [https://media.ascensionpress.com/all-bible-in-a-year-episodes/] and reading guide, [https://ascensionpress.com/pages/biy-registration]
[94] Ref 1.3 CCC 50 - 141 on revelation in general, and scripture in particular 109-119
[95] Ref 6.4 The National Catholic Education Commission (NCEC), Australian Catholic Bishops Conference. (n.d.). The Principles of Catholic Biblical Scholarship. Retrieved from Scripture for Teachers: [https://scripture.catholic.edu.au/index.php/home/foundations/catholic-biblical-interpretation/]
[96] Ref 7.1.1 Dei verbum (vatican.va) - Dogmatic Constitution on Revelation: [https://www.vatican.va/archive/hist_councils/ii_vatican_council/documents/vat-ii_const_19651118_dei-verbum_en.html]
[97] Ref 7.10 Pontifical Biblical Commission to Pope John Paul II on April 23, 1993 - as published in Origins. (1994, 1 23). The Interpretation of the Bible in the Church. Retrieved from Catholic Resources.org: [https://catholic-resources.org/ChurchDocs/PBC_Interp.htm]
[98] Ref 6.8 Fr. Mike Schmitz (for Ascension Presents). (2016, 1 12). Ways to Read the Bible. Retrieved from YouTube: [https://www.youtube.com/watch?v=6hb7nSL1gKU]

4.2.5.3　Teaching Authority (Magisterium)

Magisterium is an often-misunderstood word; it sounds like something royal or majestic, when in fact, the Latin root is 'magister', meaning 'teacher'. So then, it is a name used for the Teaching Authority of the Church which derives from Christ's authority given to the Apostles, passed on to the early Church Fathers, and inherent in the Apostolic Succession of Popes, Bishops, and Cardinals – i.e., the successors to the Apostles. [100]

Exercise of this teaching authority is most evident in the definition of *dogmas*, i.e., the proposal of "truths contained in divine revelation" or in broader terms *doctrines* proposing "in a definitive way truths having a necessary connection with them" [101] in relation to matters of faith and morals. These are held as unchanging beliefs and distinct from *disciplines* (e.g., certain liturgical forms or norms, devotions, popular expressions of piety, etc.) which, though also defined or approved within the authority of the Magisterium, are practices subject to variation or change (within the constraints of dogma and doctrine) according to custom, cultural norms, or adaptation to promote a more proper understanding and enhanced expression of the faith.

A significant portion of magisterial teaching is communicated via Church documents described earlier as comprising written forms of the 'oral' Sacred Tradition (see 4.2.5.1). Understanding the various types of documents and their relative importance can be a useful guide in the exercise of prudence with regard to their interpretation. [102]

4.3　The Relationship (Knowing Him *personally*)

"If anyone thirsts, let him come to me and drink...Whoever believes in me, ...
'Out of his heart will flow rivers of living water.' " — John 7:37-38

"Rejoice always, pray without ceasing." — 1 Thess 5:16-17

"Sicut cervus desiderat ad fontes aquarum, ita desiderat anima mea ad te, Deus."
(As a deer pants for flowing streams, so pants my soul for you, O God) [103] — Psalm 42:1

"For me, prayer is a surge of the heart; it is a simple look turned toward heaven,
it is a cry of recognition and of love, embracing both trial and joy."
— St. Therese of Lisieux [104]

"Be still, and know that I am God" — Psalm 46:10

4.3.1　We come to know Him personally in Prayer (We speak, He listens/He speaks, We listen).
4.3.2　We each pray individually in private, and we all pray together in community.
4.3.3　We grow in relationship with Him one-on-one, and as a body – the Church.
4.3.4　We grow more fully in our identity as 'human person' through this two-fold relationship.
4.3.5　We experience this relationship directly with Him and indirectly through others.
4.3.6　We experience this relationship as both immanent and transcendent to ourselves.

[99] Ref 6.9 Fr. Mike Schmitz (for Ascension Presents). (2020, 12 2). *When You Don't Understand the Bible*. Retrieved from YouTube: [https://www.youtube.com/watch?v=FNW-galVANo]
[100] Ref 7.14.1 Akin, J. (2018). Teaching with Authority: How to Cut Through Doctrinal Confusion & Understand What the Church Really Says. (Kindle edition)
[101] Ref 1.3 CCC 88
[102] Ref 7.14.2 Jimmy Akin (for Catholic Answers). (2020, 5 30). A Climb Up the Rungs of Doctrinal Authority. Retrieved from Catholic Answers: [https://www.catholic.com/magazine/print-edition/a-climb-up-the-rungs-of-doctrinal-authority]
[103] Sicut Cervus - Like the Deer that Yearns (YouTube) [https://www.youtube.com/watch?v=h2HGaJU-5Zs]
[104] Ref 1.3 CCC 2558

4.3.7   We are transformed & empowered in this relationship, both naturally & supernaturally.

4.3.8   We become one w/Him in Worship & Sacrament (We give,He receives/He gives,We receive).

4.3.8.1   *Prayer as a way of encountering, engaging and relating to God; a Way of Life*

It is said that "prayer is the raising of one's mind and heart to God..." [105]

It is the most basic and fundamental way in which we directly and personally connect with God, interact with Him, and build relationship. It is quite simply "talking to God". [106, 107]

It is the basis for acknowledging and experiencing right relationship as 'creature to Creator', as 'child to a loving Father'. We know this from God Himself, based on the answer given to a question of how to pray, in which Jesus gave what is known as "The Lord's Prayer" beginning with the words "Our Father" (with Father, translated from the Hebrew 'Abba', a most tender and endearing form, perhaps for us something more like 'Daddy'). [108]

Prayer can be in a scripted form or a more spontaneous expression. The Church has accumulated a wealth of scripted prayers which can be useful to provide a common basis across individuals in community or as a foundation on which to grow in personal prayer when unable to quite 'find the right words' on one's own. We are encouraged to utilize them, but also to grow increasingly toward personal prayer in our own voice and in our own words.

It can be done in community, or alone. It can be done out-loud verbally, or internally within one's mind and heart. In whatever form or setting, it is a relational, and as in our life experience with others, so it is with God, a dialog – speaking, and listening. Of course, "hearing God speak" is most often not a literal hearing of a voice (although this has occurred on rare occasions for some), but is more of an internal sense or notion of response; an internal movement that stirs within, that resonates with us in some way.

Much guidance is available within the Church from great Saints and mystics for properly discerning, i.e., not just listening or hearing, but also understanding and making distinctions as to authentic dialog versus 'self-talk', distraction, or even deception. This becomes increasingly important as one grows deeper in spiritual life and forms of prayer; libraries of books have been written on the subject. [109, 110, 111]

As with any interpersonal exchange, regularity, continuity, honesty, intentionality, attention, and sincerity form the basis of growth in the relationship. A shortfall in any of these areas lessens the capacity for clarity, connection, and intimacy.

It is recognized that prayer does not change God (as He is perfect and unchanging), but changes us; it may not always correspond to a change in circumstance – e.g., in the case of a request or petition – but it will often bring change to us while yet in the circumstance. This idea of transformation in and through prayer is an essential part of the experience. Our openness to God and His grace, expressed in prayer, heals our brokenness and helps us become whole, to become stronger. It helps us to recognize and grow in who we are – His beloved children, despite our imperfections – even, and especially, in the midst of life's difficulties.

Things can get in the way of prayer: distractions, busyness, fears, distorted images of God, pride, routine, illusions of self-sufficiency, etc. Our faithfulness in the face of such challenges reinforces and confirms our desire for relationship, and therefore contributes as well to our growth.

Ultimately, prayer is less something we do (or ought to do) than it is a way of being; it becomes a way of life. In fact, to live as a follower in the early Church was known as practicing "The Way". This idea, in its fullness, results in life

---

[105] Ref 1.3 CCC 2559 — St. John Damascene

[106] Ref 1.3 CCC 2558, Part 4 – Prayer, page 614 of USCCB flip-book version online:
[https://www.usccb.org/sites/default/files/flipbooks/catechism/614/]

[107] Ref 1.3 United States Catholic Catechism for Adults, Part 4 – Prayer, page 487 of flip-book version online: [
https://www.usccb.org/sites/default/files/flipbooks/uscca/files/assets/basic-html/page-487.html]

[108] Appendix - Prayers - "The Lord's Prayer – the model prayer"

[109] Ref 9.1 Acklin, F. T., & Hicks, F. B. (2019). *Personal Prayer: A Guide for Receiving the Father's Love.* (Kindle edition).

[110] Ref 8.5 Martin, R. (2006). *The Fulfillment of All Desire: A Guidebook to God Based on the Wisdom of the Saints* (Kindle Edition).

[111] Ref 8.9 Gallagher, F. T. (n.d.). *SD2 A Brief Overview of Rules 1 through 9 – Spiritual Desolation: Be Aware, Understand, Take Action with Fr. Timothy Gallagher – Discerning Hearts Podcast.* Retrieved from Discerning Hearts:[https://www.discerninghearts.com/catholic-podcasts/sd2-a-brief-overview-of-rules-1-through-9-spiritual-desolation-be-aware-understand-take-action-with-fr-timothy-gallagher-discerning-hearts-podcast/]

lived as an offering, an expression of prayer to God. It is a way of finding and acknowledging Him in all things. It is the substance and fruition of life lived in 'collaboration with God'.

4.3.8.2   *Sacraments as a way of being transformed by grace to more likeness of & unity with God*

Being incarnational creatures, i.e., a combination of both body (the material) and soul (the spiritual), we have been given means to involve both of these aspects in our expression of and growth in relationship to God. This comes in the form of what are called sacraments.

A sacrament (from the Latin roots *sacer* – sacred, *sacrare* – to hallow) is by definition as an outward (physical) sign of an inward (spiritual) reality which has been instituted by Christ to give grace, and which "efficaciously" (i.e., 'with effect') makes present what it signifies. [112, 113]

As such, sacraments facilitate the flow of grace and connection between God, through Christ and the Church, to all of mankind. The context for sacraments is the liturgy or 'work' of the Church (the "Body of Christ") centered on the Eucharist (see 6.1.4, *Engaging worship – The Mass and The Sacraments*), the key sacrament from which all others flow. In this way, the core of the sacraments is a great spiritual mystery right in the very heart of the Church, and it incorporates a transcendent, supernatural reality into the faith as lived and experienced.

4.3.8.3   *Grace and Conversion to Holiness*

Grace is by definition a gift of justification and sanctification through participation in the divine life and love of God. It is freely given, and like any gift, must be freely accepted and received in order to be effective. God initiates the gift, to which we respond and participate in relationship, to realize and bring to fruition its action and effects. The results are things which we often cannot do without God's help, but which He chooses not to do without us, i.e., without our participation. [114]

There have been various mistaken views on the notion of growing in holiness and the idea of our participation with God's grace. On one hand, it has been held that it is "all God's doing" through His grace, nothing of man's effort; on the other hand, it has been held that it is "all on us". Both of these extremes have been rejected. The Church has understood and held that God's grace enables man's response; God gives grace, and we participate with it to grow in holiness through a transformation which occurs from the "inside/out". [115]

Just as light is often used as a symbol for God's love, water often serves as a symbol for His grace. One might then think of grace as a sort of 'spiritual water', or in turn, water as 'material grace'. In either case, it is a rich analogy well worth pondering when one considers the rather unique properties of water in relation to our existence - it is essential for life, dynamic, and flowing while having clarity, purity, and as a "universal solvent", a remarkable capacity for cleansing.

The transformation to holiness, i.e., 'God-liness', is one which effects those elements at the core of our being which give us our 'likeness' to Him – in a manner of speaking, engaging both our head (intellect) and our heart (will).

---

[112] Ref 1.3 CCC 1066 - 1112

[113] Ref 1.3 CCC 1084

[114] Ref 1.3 CCC 1987 - 2029

[115] Resource 1)c) Bishop Robert Barron (for Word On Fire). (2015). *Untold Blessing: Three Paths to Holiness* (DVD and study materials). USA. [https://bookstore.wordonfire.org/collections/untold-blessing] – "...your life is not your own..."

5   The Direction

"...I came that they may have life and have it abundantly." —— *John 10:10*

*We all, with unveiled faces, are looking as in a mirror at the glory of the Lord and are
being transformed into the same image from glory to glory;
this is from the Lord who is the Spirit.* —— *2 Cor 3:18*

Our attitude and orientation determine our trajectory, the itinerary on this pilgrimage through life. These are governed by what we think (our intellect) and what we desire (our will), which in turn spur our emotions toward or away from what we want and choose to seek after. We are continually challenged to make distinctions and discern what is "of Him", i.e., sacred, versus what is "not of Him", i.e., profane.

5.1   We Follow Him, Become Like Him, and Invite Others to Do the Same
5.1.1   He gives us a perfect model and example to follow.
5.1.2   We grow to be like Him to the extent we respond, engage, & receive all we are given.
5.1.3   We help others by giving to them as we were given to.

Jesus – God the Son – gave us the perfect model and example for how to align ourselves in right relationship with God the Father and with others. With Him as our 'gold standard', we do well to turn towards Him and aim to be like Him – to know Him, love Him, think like Him, see as He sees, love as He loves, want what He wants...and we know (because He told us) that He wants what the Father wants. To be aligned in the right direction is to be aligned with His will, and thus in turn, the Fathers will – and because He and the Father love us beyond all measure, it will ultimately be what is best for us, and for those around us. Perhaps it will not always be easy or pleasant in the short term, but it will for sure lead to Him, the best possible long-term outcome.

We respond through prayer, through our decisions and actions, through discernment, and through aligning our will with God's perfect will. Relationship with God the Father is the primary goal, Jesus the Son is the Way to that goal, and the Holy Spirit is the means and motivation for living that goal. More properly stated, it is less a goal to achieve, than it is a gift to receive.

It is fundamentally about allowing ourselves to be "Spirit filled" and "Spirit led". [116, 117, 118]

To do this directs us toward loving God, and loving others. It then, likewise, leads us to help others turn in the same direction.

The Holy Spirit is our primary advocate, though we are not entirely subject to influence by Him alone in this endeavor; there are also other lesser though significant spiritual advocates and adversaries that attempt to keep us on track or move us off course.

---

[116] Ref 1.1 ESV John 14:15-19
[117] Ref 1.1 ESV Isaiah 11:1-3 Gifts of the Spirit
[118] Ref 1.1 ESV Galatians 5:22-23 Fruit of the Spirit

5.2 We Seek All That is Of Him (Holiness)
As we say 'yes' to righteousness, obedience, and fullness of life, we will find assistance.

5.2.1   Some spiritual beings (Angels - 7.1.4) accept service to God & support us.

5.2.2   They facilitate influence consistent with God; our cooperation draws us closer to Him.

5.2.3   We are vulnerable on our own, but are promised their assistance, with God's grace.

5.3 We Reject All That is Not Of Him (Evil)
As we say 'no' to sin, disobedience, and death, we will find opposition.

5.3.1   Some spiritual beings (Demons, "fallen angels"-7.1.4) reject service to God & oppose us.

5.3.2   They facilitate influence contrary to God; our cooperation moves us away from Him.

5.3.3   We are vulnerable on our own, but are promised to overcome them, with God's grace.

The notion of a sort of spiritual 'tug-of-war' between good and evil has been with us throughout the ages, and has been often caricatured in popular culture with the iconic angel [119] on one shoulder and demon [120] on the other. Nevertheless, the reality of this tension is something we all experience, and effects of our response to these influences are evidenced all around us. While a purely materialistic view would dismiss the existence of such influences as spiritual beings and would seek to explain them away as purely psychological or physiological phenomena, such existence would appear to be held or at least deemed plausible across a wide range of people (and arguably, a majority) who have even the most casual of spiritual interest and inclination.

Within the perspective suggest here, such influences are at play in nearly every circumstance of life, both the apparently mundane and significant. If one considers life lived as an expression of one's values, beliefs, and desires, each decision moves the trajectory of one's path either closer to God, i.e., all that is true, good, and beautiful, or further in the other direction. Simple things like choices of entertainment (music, movies, sports, etc.), hobbies, leisure, socializing, or various communications, whether spoken, written, via print or social media, etc. all cumulatively combine to build a pattern and profile of one's outlook – in a sense, what we are pursuing and presenting (either consciously or unconsciously; intentionally or mindlessly) and why, as a picture of "what we are about".

In many dimensions, there is room for integration and combination of varying and diverse things, but in some dimensions, there are oppositions which cannot be combined or reconciled – for example and most significantly, things like light/dark, good/evil, caring love/indifference. To the extent that our lived picture of "what we are about" – fashioned in some way based upon our response to the above spiritual influences – aligns with the nature of God, we prepare ourselves to draw close to Him in relationship, or to drift apart from Him.

As a result, the most relevant question for us moment to moment becomes "is this of God and will it draw me closer to Him, or is this not of God and will it move me further away from Him"?

---

[119] Ref 8.18 Tadié, S. (2020, 9 29). *Renowned Angel Expert Explains Amazing Facts Every Catholic Should Know About Angels*. Retrieved from National Catholic Register: [https://www.ncregister.com/blog/angels-101]

[120] Ref 8.17 Adam Blai (for EWTN). (2016, 01 02). *EWTN On Location - Exorcism In The Modern Church And How To Keep The Doors To The Demonic Closed*. Retrieved from YouTube: [https://www.youtube.com/watch?v=JKnGdr9WMqs]

6   The Path

I appeal to you therefore, brothers, by the mercies of God, to present your bodies as a living sacrifice, holy and acceptable to God, which is your spiritual worship. Do not be conformed to this world, but be transformed by the renewal of your mind, that by testing you may discern what is the will of God, what is good and acceptable and perfect.
—— Romans 12:1-2

"Through Him, and With Him, and in Him..."
Final Doxology of the Eucharistic Prayer[121]

14 What good is it, my brothers, if someone says he has faith but does not have works? Can that faith save him? If a brother or sister is poorly clothed and lacking in daily food, 16 qand one of you says to them, "Go in peace, be warmed and filled," without giving them the things needed for the body, what good2 is that? 17 So also faith by itself, if it does not have works, is dead.
— James 2:14-17

Preparing to move, then moving along the path becomes a life-long process; equipping and grounding oneself in Him and the life that He offers...and eventually picking up, joining with, and bringing others along on the journey. Moving along this path is less about implementing a plan or ascribing to a philosophy, than it is engaging and living in the context of a particular personal relationship and the community which flows from it.

Even the smallest of steps, taken regularly and sincerely (even if only tentatively), become the seeds and expression of "faith seeking understanding" (St. Anselm).

6.1   Be Open and Grow in Faith, Hope, and Love on the Inside

---

Be still, and know that I am God
— Psalm 46:10

6.1.1   Know and be known with Him in the silence and intimacy of Prayer
6.1.2   Connect and grow with Him in the depth and richness Scripture
6.1.3   Connect and live with Him in the secure context of Tradition.
6.1.4   Unite & be transformed by Him & His Church in the communion of Worship & Sacrament

Engaging prayer is fundamental to growing in faith.

---

[121] Ref 1.3 CCC 1065, 1553

A regular, daily habit of 15 minutes or more of dedicated prayer can lay a foundation and set the tone for a day of life lived in faith, and inevitably grows over time to become central.

Praying is essentially communicating with God (see 4.3.8.1), and there are three basic ways to do it: 1) vocal (speaking, singing to), 2) meditation (pondering, reflecting on), and 3) contemplation (being, resting with). In whatever method or setting, the aim is to seek full personal engagement of mind, body, heart, and soul in relation to God. Praise and worship are other more expressive, moving, even at times exuberant ways to engage God [122] whereas, prayer is a more settled, collected, and interior connection. It is said that God speaks to us in the silence of our hearts [123], and silence remains a consistent theme among the most learned and experienced of those who have trod this path before us.

There are many examples of prayer one may explore. [124, 125, 126] There are basic types of prayer which fall into one or several general categories: blessings, adoration, petition, intercession, thanksgiving, and praise.

See (Appendix - **Prayers**) for a few that are essential and widely prayed.

One of the most effective ways to grow deeper in personal, private prayer is Eucharistic Adoration, simply spending time in the presence of the Lord in the Eucharist. [127] Many speak of profound, deeply moving personal experiences deriving from a 'holy hour' spend in front of the Blessed Sacrament.

Engaging scripture is fundamental to growing in faith.

A regular, daily habit of reading and reflecting on at least few lines of scripture (perhaps the daily readings for mass or similar from a devotional) provides a direct connection to 'the source' of our faith. According to St. Jerome, a father and Doctor of the Church from the 5th century AD, "ignorance of Scripture is ignorance of Christ".[128] The opposite holds as well; knowledge of Scripture becomes knowledge of Christ. [129]

Scripture is perhaps most fruitful when it is read and reflected upon in the context of prayer, which then becomes a dialog since Scripture is understood to embody the inspired, living Word of God. This can take many forms, e.g.,

- o Psalms, the prayer book/hymnal of the Bible [130]
- o Liturgy of the Word during Mass
  - Daily Devotional with Mass readings [131, 132]
- o Liturgy of the Hours (Prayer of the Church", also known as the "Divine Office") [133, 134]
  - Morning and Evening Prayer
- o Lectio Divina (Divine Reading – "praying with Scripture") [135, 136]
  (Divine Reading, praying with/thru scripture and/or as a general roadmap for prayer):
  - Lectio (Read)   Prayer as engaging, connecting

---

[122] Resource 35) The Vigil Project [https://www.thevigilproject.com/]

[123] Ref 1.3 pages 479-480, Meditation – "I Shall Keep the Silence of My Heart", Mother Teresa [https://www.usccb.org/sites/default/files/flipbooks/uscca/files/assets/basic-html/page-507.html]

[124] Ref 9.5 [https://catholic-link.org/images/gallery-10-ways-to-pray/]

[125] Ref 9.6 [http://www.usccb.org/prayer-and-worship/prayers-and-devotions/prayers/]

[126] Ref 9.3 Hallow – prayer and meditation app [https://hallow.com]

[127] Ref 3.8 3.8. Kristen Aebli (for Catholic Exchange). (2017, 9 28). One Thing Adoration. Retrieved from Catholic Exchange: https://catholicexchange.com/one-thing-adoration/

[128] Ref 1.3 CCC 133

[129] Resources 4)b) and 4)c) Fr. Mike Schmitz, Bible in a Year podcast, [https://media.ascensionpress.com/all-bible-in-a-year-episodes/] and reading guide, [https://ascensionpress.com/pages/biy-registration]

[130] Ref 9.7 A video montage introducing fundamental concepts of prayer, particularly the Psalms which cover the entire range of human experience and emotion: Dan Stevers - Prayer Intro [https://www.youtube.com/watch?v=C5S2flwltts&list=PLtS8Xw9v7kRdp4brbPAo9HoDhCnEaklxx&index=3]

[131] Magnificat (online) [https://us.magnificat.net/home/onlineIssue]

[132] Word Among Us (online) [https://wau.org/archives/40-07/]

[133] Universalis (online) [www.universalis.com]

[134] iBreviary (online) [https://www.ibreviary.org/en/ibreviary/what-is-the-ibreviary.html]

[135] Ref 9.8 [https://www.ncregister.com/tag/lectio-divina]

[136] Ref 9.9 [https://www.usccb.org/prayer-and-worship/prayers-and-devotions/meditations]

- Meditatio (Meditate)   Prayer as reflecting, considering
- Oratio (Pray)   Prayer as expressing, relating
- Contemplatio (Contemplate)   Prayer as being with
- Actio (Act)   Prayer as doing

Engaging tradition is fundamental to growing in faith.

A regular habit of reading and consulting the Catechism (and corresponding internal references to scripture, Church documents, etc.) provides a deepened context for growth in the faith, and provides a stable foundation from which insights can be gained and shared. [137, 138]

If "ignorance of scripture is ignorance of Christ",[139] it could be said that 'ignorance of the Catechism is ignorance of the Church'. As the Church is understood to be the 'Body of Christ', by extension, a lack of familiarity with the Church teaches and why is a gap in understanding Christ most fully.

Venerable Fulton Sheen is claimed to have made the observation that "There are not one hundred people in the United States who hate the Catholic Church, but there are millions who hate what they wrongly perceive the Catholic Church to be."

Growing in at least familiarity with the Catechism has become an increasingly important staple in remaining grounded in the faith, and foundational in being able to live and profess the faith in the modern world. This is especially so given the pervasive array of misconceptions and distortions which stand in the way of understanding – both inside and outside the walls of the Church. How unfortunate that a transformative relationship with God through the Church can be impacted by someone's misbegotten views or representations of Him and His Church.

It is tempting to think that this is a new and different sort of challenge, but it has always been so from the very beginning. Having the Catechism at hand is a distinct advantage in addressing the particular challenges of our day and time. [140]

Engaging worship – The Mass and The Sacraments – is at the heart of growing in faith [141]

The summary list below identifies in brief the sacramental means by which grace is made manifest in the heart of the Church. Each in their own way conveys to us Christs love and mercy, visibly and tangibly at various points in our life. They all flow from the most central of all sacraments, the Eucharist – Christ Himself, mystically made present on the altar at every celebration of the Mass. [142, 143]

While each sacrament provides a sense of witness and includes elements of healing, they are not primarily evangelistic nor therapeutic, but instead in their essence – to the extent the disposition of our hearts is open to it – transformational. This holds true regardless the particular style and expression of liturgical setting, or the personal sanctity of the mediating priest.

- Sacraments of Initiation (each occurs once in a lifetime)
  - Baptism: water, chrism, white garment, candle
  - Confirmation: chrism, laying on of hands
- Sacrament of The Eucharist (repeats) [144]
  - Bread & wine become Body & Blood, Soul & Divinity of Christ

---

[137] CCC and scripture 'read-in-a-year' guide from Coming Home Network [https://chnetwork.org/free-resource-updated-version-of-our-read-the-bible-and-the-catechism-in-a-year-guide/]

[138] Ref 4)d) Catechism in a Year Podcast [https://ascensionpress.com/pages/catechisminayear]

[139] Ref 1.3 CCC 133

[140] Ref 7.9 Fidei Depositum (Vatican.va) – Deposit of Faith: [https://www.vatican.va/content/john-paul-ii/en/apost_constitutions/documents/hf_jp-ii_apc_19921011_fidei-depositum.html] In section IV, 'The Doctrinal Value of the Text', St. John Paul II declares that the Catechism of the Catholic Church is a "sure norm for teaching the faith".

[141] Ref 1.3 CCC 1113 - 1114

[142] Ref 10.3 Barron, B. R. (2020, 02 27). *The Real Presence of Jesus in the Eucharist // Bishop Barron at 2020 Religious Education Congress.* Retrieved from YouTube: [https://www.youtube.com/watch?v=UzCPu_IEhe8]

[143] Ref 10.4 Dr. Ray Guarendi. (2020, 11 16). *Why Be Catholic? | Full Movie,* segment on the Eucharist – The Quarter (29:40 – 35:41) Retrieved from YouTube: [https://www.youtube.com/embed/faZV--bkiGY?start=1919&end=2141]

[144] Ref 1.3 CCC 1322 - 1419

- o Sacraments of Healing (repeats)
    - Reconciliation: confession, contrition, absolution [amendment] [145]
    - Anointing of the Sick: oil, laying on of hands, prayer
- o Sacraments of Service (exclusively, and once in a lifetime)
    - Matrimony: vows, consummation
    - Holy Orders: oil, laying on of hands, garment, vows

Even those regularly practicing the faith have faced in various ways and in various times challenges to participation in the sacramental life of the Church. More than ever, appreciation for the immense gift of the Eucharist and the sustenance it brings has heightened. At the same time, there is an ever-present temptation to take it for granted, along with the other Sacraments, not fully appreciating the encounter with Christ inherent within each one of them. It is useful to consider how things might be different were we to grow in knowledge, understanding, and awe of these incredible, supernatural gifts of grace. What if the faithful began to live more fully and authentically in the reality of what the sacraments bring to us in these distinct and potentially powerful moments of our lives?

The sacraments are at once both the incarnational and supernatural means by which we are nourished and fed – the means by which the Lord gives us all that we need to endure in our day-to-day struggles as we seek to grow closer to Him, and deeper in holiness and participation in His divine life, bringing Him into our lives and all of the lives that we touch.

6.2   Be Real and Express Faith, Hope, and Love on the Outside
Redeem and offer oneself, in service of and invitation to Him in the life that He offers, both now and in eternity. [146]

6.2.1   We offer to others, in service to Him, support of their needs of the body (Corporal Works)
6.2.2   We offer to others, in service to Him, support of their needs of the soul (Spiritual Works)
6.2.3   We use sacramentals as tangible reminders and indications of our faith and devotion.
6.2.4   We invite others to participate in the same fullness of relationship and destiny with God.

The following list outlines a set of 'works' that are traditionally held to be the means by which Christians carry out the imperative to love God, and by extension, love and serve others:

Corporal	Spiritual
Feed the Hungry	Admonish the Sinner
Give Drink to the Thirsty	Instruct the Ignorant
Clothe the Naked	Counsel the Doubtful
Shelter the Homeless	Comfort the Sorrowful
Visit the Imprisoned	Bear Wrongs Patiently
Visit the Sick	Forgive all Injuries
Bury the Dead	Pray for the Living & the Dead

Table 1 - Works of Mercy

These so-called 'Works of Mercy' [147] fall into two categories which address the entirety of the human-person, namely both body ('corporal') and soul ('spiritual'). Carrying them forward in service to others makes the love of God both known and present to them (and us as well) in whatever circumstance.

---

[145] Resource 31)a) Burke-Sivers, D. H. (2016, 8 24). *Gathering of Catholic Men 2015*, segment on Reconciliation (13:13 – 25:05). Retrieved from YouTube: [https://www.youtube.com/embed/nbU8ZeileOY?start=793&end=1494]
[146] Ref 2)a) Kenosis and associated titles – from Anima, a three-part production on the life of faith [https://www.ahavaproductions.com/anima]
[147] Resource 8)g) The Wonders of His Mercy, Fr Wade Menezes - Episode 4: THE 14 WORKS OF MERCY [https://www.youtube.com/watch?v=kJyDWhg9390]

Sacramentals [148] are sacred signs bearing resemblance to sacraments which signify spiritual effects ("blessings", holiness) obtained through the intercession of the Church. They do not confer the grace of the Holy Spirit (as sacraments do), but dispose an openness to it.

6.3   Be Aware of Opposition
Recognize there are influences (internal and external) opposed to Him and the life He offers.

"...the light has come into the world,
and people loved the darkness rather than the light..."
— John 3:19

6.3.1   We are subject to deception and response to influence contrary to God.

6.3.2   We thus contribute to growth of disorder, sin, sickness, & death in material creation.

6.3.3   We thus contribute to growth of defect, blemish, stain, & corruption in spiritual creation.

6.3.4   We thus damage and sometimes break our right order of relationship to God & others.

6.3.5   We experience this challenge of influence contrary to God as life-long struggle.

6.3.6   We can grow in ability to recognize deception by cooperating with God & His grace.

6.3.7   We can grow in ability to reject contrary influence by cooperating with God & His grace.

6.3.8   He gave us a means for reconciling broken relationship through, with, and in His Church.

Moving along the path in the right direction in the spiritual live is not without its challenges, partly because of the remaining weaknesses and tendencies within us, but also because the path brings various forms of distractions and obstacles, and as discussed earlier in sections 5.2 and 5.3, we are not alone on the path. A popular tag line says "it's all good", but half or more of the struggle is recognizing that, in fact, "it ain't all good". [149, 150, 151]

So, the first step to engage in the struggle against adverse influences (internal and external) opposed to Him and the life that He offers is to recognize they exist. Not to become overly concerned or hype-sensitive, looking for evil influences around every corner or in every thought or emotion, nor to have a nonchalant or dismissive attitude, but to have a healthy and realistic awareness and vigilance. The next step is to grow in capability to recognize them and avoid being deceived, i.e., discerning that which is of Him, and that which is not of Him. [152, 153]

Once discerned, we have all of the power of prayer, the Holy Spirit, and sacramental grace in relationship to God to strengthen us in choosing light and life over darkness and death. When we fail, we have the opportunity to repent and the particular means for restoration in the grace of the Sacrament of Reconciliation (Confession). We also have the assistance, guidance, and support of those surrounding us in the faith as we continue to move forward.

---

[148] Ref 1.3 CCC 1667 - 1676
[149] Ref 1.1 ESV 1 John 5:16-17
[150] Ref 1.3 CCC 1854 - 1864
[151] Ref 5.9 Therrien, M. (2020). The Catholic Faith Explained – "13. The Problem of Evil"
[152] Ref 8.8 Bishop Robert Barron (for Word on Fire with Brandon Vogt). (2019, 11 11). *How to Discern the Spirits.* Retrieved from YouTube: [https://www.youtube.com/watch?v=jzYN2hMqLI4]
[153] Ref 8.9 Gallagher, F. T. (n.d.). *SD2 A Brief Overview of Rules 1 through 9 – Spiritual Desolation: Be Aware, Understand, Take Action with Fr. Timothy Gallagher – Discerning Hearts Podcast.* Retrieved from Discerning Hearts:[https://www.discerninghearts.com/catholic-podcasts/sd2-a-brief-overview-of-rules-1-through-9-spiritual-desolation-be-aware-understand-take-action-with-fr-timothy-gallagher-discerning-hearts-podcast/]

7   The Support

"Therefore, since we are surrounded by so great a cloud of witnesses, let us also lay aside every weight, and sin which clings so closely, and let us run with endurance the race that is set before us..."
----- *Hebrews 12:1*

"I do not ask for these only, but also for those who will believe in me through their word, that they may all be one, just as you, Father, are in me, and I in you, that they also may be in us, so that the world may believe that you have sent me."
----- *John 17:20*

7.1   Our Mentors and Guardians
We have assistance in those who have gone before us and those who go before us spiritually.

7.1.1   Those human beings who have gone before us & lived exemplary lives are our mentors.

7.1.2   Some mentors are formally recognized as Saints worthy to admire and aspire to.

7.1.3   Saints are with God, are for us, and can intercede in prayer on our behalf upon request.

7.1.4   Angels are spiritual beings created before us who live in service to God, with and for us.

7.1.5   A specific angel is assigned to each one of us to serve as our guardian throughout our life.

7.1.6   Angels are with God (thus, also Saints) and can intercede and act on our behalf.

We live in a time when all things past are often viewed with suspicion at worst or apathy at best, yet past experiences are of profound importance in understanding many truths and life principals. It is a great loss when they are overlooked or dismissed, and it summons a quote from an iconic figure who is said to have once suggested: "Become better informed. Lean from others' mistakes. You could not live long enough to make them all yourself."

This would seem to ring true as well with respect to the revelation and perennial wisdom of the ages passed on within and through the Church. It takes a degree of humility and perspective to benefit from the richness of Tradition and learn from those who have gone before us.

In the case of those determined to be Saints, [154, 155] we have not only the opportunity to learn from their experience, inspirations, and writings within Tradition (see 4.2.5.1), but also to further engage them here and now by asking for their prayers and assistance. As we understand them to be in Heaven, near to God and rather more alive spiritually than ever, we can ask their special intercession in much the same way we would a friend or loved one living here now with us.

---

[154] Ref 8.5 Martin, R. (2006). *The Fulfillment of All Desire: A Guidebook to God Based on the Wisdom of the Saints* (Kindle Edition).

[155] Resource 11)d)i) O'Neill, M. (2021). *They Might Be Saints: On the Path to Sainthood in America.*

We can do similarly for our guardian angels, known to be assigned to us by virtue of words from Christ himself. [156] Often misconceived in childhood devotion as cute little cherub-like figures, angels are powerful intercessors and would present an awe-inspiring, and perhaps intimidating presence if made fully known and visible to us. [157]

See (Appendix - **Saints**) for an index to a number of notable Saints and links to biographical and information concerning the many prayer intentions and devotional practices with which they are associated.

7.2 Our Immediate Family
We have assistance in those who accompany us on the path – all of us, 'saints in the making'.

7.2.1   Those human beings who are here with us now living are all our brothers and sisters.
7.2.2   Some brothers and sisters seek to live life in close relationship to God and can assist us.
7.2.3   We serve God when we seek to live saintly lives bringing others to Him and Him to others.
7.2.4   The Church is the community in which such saintly lives are encouraged and nourished.
7.2.5   The Church embodies His Legacy (see 4) and provides us Means in our Mission (see 3.3)
7.2.6   We thus bring light, love, order, & right relationship into this life & carry it into eternity.

Flowing from the gospel teachings, there is a call for all to "holiness" [158] - in a manner of speaking, a call to 'be a saint' - for all the faithful.

All those now living who share in this endeavor reflect in their own unique way the image and likeness of God in which they are made, and which dwells within them by virtue of their participation in the sacramental life. These are, in a sense, 'living icons' [159], often everyday folks who point to Him in their own particular way, or in some cases more visibly leading [160] and drawing people toward Him in dynamic [161, 162] and sometimes surprising ways. [163, 164, 165, 166]

Taken together, the individual lives of all these aspiring 'saints' makes present the 'Body of Christ' - the name given to the Church which is perhaps most descriptive. With Christ as founder and 'head', and the individuals can be thought of as the 'cells' of this mystical body. By extension, Christ designated Peter to stand in this role of authority when he stated "You are Peter, and on this rock, I will build my church". [167]

See (Appendix - **Structure of the Church**) for a brief overview of some general organizational aspects of the Church, and examples of religious life]

---

[156] Ref 1.1 ESV Matt 18:10,
[157] Ref 8.18 Tadié, S. (2020, 9 29). *Renowned Angel Expert Explains Amazing Facts Every Catholic Should Know About Angels*. Retrieved from National Catholic Register: [https://www.ncregister.com/blog/angels-101]
[158] Ref 1.3 CCC 2013 - 2016
[159] Resource 8)d) Icons [https://ondemand.ewtn.com/free/Home/Series/ondemand/video/en/icons] - see this series for examples.
[160] Resource 34) The Culture Project; [https://thecultureproject.org/]
[161] Resource 7) Dynamic Catholic [https://www.dynamiccatholic.com/]
[162] Resource 24) FOCUS – Fellowship of Catholic University Students [https://www.focus.org/]
[163] Resource 12)b) Real Life Catholic - Holy Dirt [https://www.facebook.com/ewtnonline/videos/real-life-catholic-holy-dirt/10154797804202582/]
[164] Resource 12)a) Real Life Catholic [https://www.youtube.com/channel/UC9Gin8zVjjzywF_sW9fkODA]
[165] Resource 25)a) Hard as Nails Ministries [https://www.youtube.com/watch?v=L38rwpU_4Rk&list=PL-UqJ3ASAgHg2E1ep7xPp79vPfs-KBe1W&index=10]
[166] Resource 25) Hard as Nails Ministries [https://www.amazingnation.org/]
[167] Ref 1.1 ESV Matt 16:13-19, in particular verse Matt 16:18

7.3   Our Extended Family [168]

We accompany all faithful and join in outreach to the world in hope, that eventually that we 'may all be one' in Him. [169]

7.3.1   God came to save all mankind and expressed a desire for unity among all people.

7.3.2   Influences contrary to God have arisen in history introducing errors in teaching & belief.

7.3.3   Influences contrary to God have facilitated division, splits, and fragmentation.

7.3.4   The Church remained essentially one for nearly 1000 years before an East/West break.

7.3.5   The Church experienced the next major split in the 1500's, first of many continuing today.

7.3.6   The Church seeks to draw all separated brethren into unity of faith, if not in expression.

7.3.7   The Church seeks to draw all of mankind into right relationship with God and each other.

As a result of influences contrary to God (see 6.3) and the reality that, this side of heaven the holiness of the Church is carried forward within fallible, imperfect human beings ("earthen vessels" – see 3.3), there have been from the beginning and throughout history, deviations from authentic faith (heresies), scandals, corruption, etc. As a result there has been over the centuries a progression of fragmentation and splits into various denominations [170, 171] with corresponding misconceptions, distortions, and myths [172] often motivated by worldly considerations and influences.

The various divisions among separated Christian brothers and sisters of faith have regrettably caused confusion and impacted the effectiveness of witness to the wider world of non-believers. Nevertheless, though substantive differences remain to be resolved, there is a wide agreement on many principals held in common from which progress continues to be made.

A recurrent theme of 'both/and' in regards to elements of truth which need to be held in balance and tension (e.g., truth and love, faith and reason, justice and mercy, etc.) can be more than instrumental in any approach to ecumenical dialog across denominations – or even, dialog between groupings having polarized perspectives amidst a particular branch of the faith, an ever increasingly common circumstance.

Despite all this, the Church retains a sacred foundation and remains holy in its essence, guided by the Holy Spirit, seeking to draw all to faith and unity. [173]

---

[168] Ref 1.3 CCC 816 - 822, 836 - 856

[169] Ref 1.1 ESV John 17:20

[170] Ref 4.3 Denominations Comparison pamphlet. (2003). Rose Publishing, Inc.

[171] Ref 4.5 Moczar, D. (2013). The Church Under Attack: Five Hundred Years That Split the Church and Scattered the Flock. Manchester, NH: Sophia Institute Press.

[172] Ref 4.6 Moczar, D. (2010). Seven Lies About Catholic History. Charlotte, NC: TAN Books (Kindle edition).

[173] Ref 1.1 ESV John 17:20-23..."that they may be one";
He died for all (2 Cor 5:15, 2 Tim 2:12, Col 1:20, 1 John 2:2, Rom 1:16, Heb 5:9)

8   The Goal

What no eye has seen, nor ear heard, nor the heart of man imagined,
what God has prepared for those who love him.
— *1 Cor 2:9*

"In my Father's house are many rooms. If it were not so, would I have told you
that I go to prepare a place for you? And if I go and prepare a place for you, I will
come again and will take you to myself, that where I am you may be also."
— *John 14:2-3*

8.1   Wholeness

"The glory of God is man fully alive, but the life of man is the vision of God."
— *St. Irenaeus*

"But thanks be to God, who in Christ always leads us in triumphal procession,
and through us spreads the fragrance of the knowledge of him everywhere.
— *2 Corinthians 2:14*

8.1.1   We integrate both aspects of our humanity, body & soul, in our expression of life & love.

8.1.2   We experience wholeness when in alignment with what is true, good, and beautiful.

8.1.3   We experience fullness of life when we are in right relationship with God and others.

8.1.4   We find grounding for wholeness and fullness of life in attributes of holiness.

Our worldly existence this side of heaven is full of natural tensions between what appear to be opposites but are instead to be understood and lived as complementary: corporal and spiritual, "vertical and horizontal" relationship/worship, active and contemplative. [174]

To the extent we come to realize that the theme of life lived in faith is more often a "both/and" than "either/or", that realization brings us the capability to truly have it all and be it all, though maybe not always precisely at the same time and in the same place. Even still, the possibility unfolds for things like joy in the midst of suffering, beauty in the

---

[174] Ref 8.6 Chautard, J.-B. (1946, 2008). The Soul of the Apostolate - Part Two, "Union of the Active Life and the Interior Life"

31

midst of challenge, wisdom born of disappointment and defeat – often yielding the moments of transformation, revelation, and growth that would not have otherwise been possible in the "best" of circumstances.

This unfolding may appear to us random, and there is to be sure an element of spontaneity and creativity, however the broad stretch of time and human experience brings a view of clear pattern and purpose – not only in a collective way for all of us together, but also for each of us in a particular, individual way. What is even more intriguing is that we can gain this perspective in the 'now' of each moment of our lives if we are willing to be open and enter into the kind of relationships we are invited to, and to see ourselves as what we truly are - incredibly gifted creatures within the extraordinary order of a vast and purposeful creation. [175]

There is a special path unique for each one of us, and we can gain 'real-time' insights into it – not necessarily the complete picture, but at least the next few steps for us to take – if we are open to receiving it. [176]

8.2   Peace and Joy

"The person God loves with the tenderness of a Father, the person he wants to touch and to transform with his love, is not the person we'd have liked to be or ought to be. It's the person we are. God doesn't love "ideal persons" or "virtual beings." He loves actual, real people...A great deal of time can be wasted in the spiritual life complaining that we are not like this or not like that, lamenting this defect or that limitation...a waste of time and energy that merely impedes the work of the Holy Spirit in our hearts."
— Jacques Phillippe, Interior Freedom [177]

"...whatever is true, whatever is honorable, whatever is just, whatever is pure, whatever is lovely, whatever is commendable, if there is any excellence, if there is anything worthy of praise, think about these things.
What you have learned and received and heard and seen in me — practice these things, and the God of peace will be with you."
— Philippians 4:8-9

8.2.1	We experience 'happiness' (i.e., peace & joy), through holiness, right relation with God.
8.2.2	We experience unfulfillment (i.e., emptiness & angst) in worldly things apart from God.
8.2.3	We are commonly deceived by counterfeits of power, prestige, pleasure, & possessions.
8.2.4	We are commonly misled by attractions focused inward on self, vs outward toward others.

We experience a 'fullness of fulfillment' when we seek connectedness, not empty isolation. [178]

We begin to ask, perhaps for the first time, more fundamental questions: what are you doing, how are you doing it, why are you doing it, who are you doing it for (not what we might try to convince ourselves of, but *really*), who are you doing it with...? [179]

---

[175] Ref 8.2.1 Dr. Stacy Trasancos for (Steubenville Conferences). (2019, 9 27). Dr. Stacy Trasancos - The Faith and Science Conflict Myth (2019 Defending the Faith Conference). Retrieved from YouTube – excerpt (56:02 – 01:09:32), "Photosynthesis" https://www.youtube.com/embed/upAjw3YO7n4?start=3362&end=4172

[176] Ref 8.10 One Billion Stories. (2019, 6 19). *Don Briel: a Life of Purpose and Joy* – opening segment on Newman (0:02 – 1.32)
Retrieved from YouTube: [https://www.youtube.com/embed/Xz7qiSeEISc?start=2&end=92]

[177] Ref 8.7 page 32, Philippe, Jacques (2007). *Interior Freedom*. New York, NY: Scepter Publishers, Inc.

[178] Ref 5.13 Spitzer, F. R. (2017). *Big Book* - Credible Catholic [https://www.crediblecatholic.com/big-book/] - Volume 13 – FOUR LEVELS OF HAPPINESS [https://www.crediblecatholic.com/pdf/7E-P6/7E-BB13.pdf#P1V13]

[179] Ref 8.11 Joseph, M. (2018). Overwhelming Pursuit: Stop Chasing Your Life and Live.

Those who have done so and discovered their 'special path' suggest finding fulfillment that had previously been elusive. In the process, self-reliance and vice give way to humility and virtue, bringing contentment, peace, and joy [180] – even in the midst of challenge, effort, and struggle. [181, 182]

We are all 'works in progress' and in terms of this discovery, the 'sooner the better', though it is never too late in this life to prepare for the next. [183]

3.3 Eternity

Let nothing disturb you,
Let nothing frighten you,
All things are passing away;
God never changes.
Patience obtains all things.
Whoever has God lacks nothing;
God alone suffices.
— St Teresa of Avila

"For God so loved the world, that he gave his only Son, that whoever believes in him should not perish but have eternal life. For God did not send his Son into the world to condemn the world, but in order that the world might be saved through him. Whoever believes in him is not condemned, but whoever does not believe is condemned already, because he has not believed in the name of the only Son of God. And this is the judgment: the light has come into the world, and people loved the darkness rather than the light because their works were evil.
For everyone who does wicked things hates the light and does not come to the light, lest his works should be exposed. But whoever does what is true comes to the light, so that it may be clearly seen that his works have been carried out in God."
— John 3:16-21

3.3.1   We live life as integrated body & soul, but on death, our soul will separate from the body.

3.3.2   We will encounter Him at the moment of death and experience our particular judgement.

3.3.3   We will experience the fullness of God's justice and mercy.

3.3.4   Our soul will experience an ultimate eternal destiny with God, or separated from Him.

3.3.5   At the end of time, Jesus will again return to earth for a general judgement of all mankind.

3.3.6   Our bodies will be resurrected in glorified form and reunited with our soul.

3.3.7   We hope to experience eternal glory in the presence of God & loved ones forever after.

The beginning of 'the Fall' and the ending of 'Salvation History' culminates for all of us and each of us in the context of relationship. We are reconciled in and through Christ, as "...God so loved the world..." [184] and we live our lives as 'pilgrim' disciples on mission[185], journeying to our eternal home. [186, 187]

---

[180] Ref 8.14 Centricity Worship. (2014, 9 15). *Lauren Daigle - "Come Alive (Dry Bones) (Live at the CentricWorship Retreat)*. Retrieved from YouTube: [https://www.youtube.com/watch?v=7XAeyFagceQ]

[181] Ref 8.20 HM Television (English). (2016, 11 14). All or Nothing: Sr. Clare Crockett - Official Trailer. Retrieved from YouTube: https://www.youtube.com/watch?v=N7sBW-cnWgA

[182] Ref 8.19 FrassatiUSA. (2016, 4 17). PGF (Per Giorgio Frassati) get to know him TEASER. Retrieved from YouTube: https://www.youtube.com/watch?v=bagWsNLOIOI&

[183] Ref 1.1 ESV Philippians 1:6,

[184] Ref 1.1 ESV John 3:16-21

[185] Ref 28) MTYR - You are More Than You Realize [https://mtyr.org/]

[186] Ref 1.3 CCC 1051 - 1060

A point of transition we know as physical death [188, 189] awaits at the end of this life, and brings us finally into direct face-to-face encounter with our God. [190, 191, 192] In this moment, the destiny for which we have been preparing and fo which we have chosen in each and every point of decision expressed in our lives will come to fulfillment (perhaps afte some final preparation [193, 194, 195]) in one of two ways: union [196, 197] or separation. [198, 199, 200]

We have been given a sense of what the expectations will be in this encounter,[201] and the essential consideration will be response to the core of His teachings from section 4.1.1 – love of God and love of neighbor. One migh anticipate a basic two-part query: 1) "What did you do with the blessings I gave you?" and 2) "Who did you bring with you?", or in other words "who did you introduce to Me and invite into my Church?"

We have been given glimpses of the pain and loss of rejection of God's grace and eternal separation.[202, 203] It is fa more and far worse than anything we have experienced or can imagine. We have likewise been given glimpses of the glory of union with God in what is called Heaven. [204, 205]

It is far more and far better than anything we have experienced or can imagine.

---

[187] Crux of the Matter - 4 Last Things, Fr Wade Menezes-Video: [
https://www.youtube.com/watch?v=61aFHKl1vtw]

[188] Ref 1.3 CCC 1006 - 1020

[189] Ref 1.1 ESV John 3:16-21, Romans 5:12

[190] Ref 8.12 Fr. Agustino Torres, CFR (for EWTN); (2018). *Icons - 2018-10-26 - Place in Presence* – opening segment (0:00 – 1:05) Retrieved from YouTube: [https://www.youtube.com/embed/4hPQEtY_tNw?start=0&end=65]

[191] Ref 1.3 CCC 678 - 682, 1021 - 1022, 1038 - 1041

[192] Ref 1.1 ESV Luke 15:19-31, Eccl 12:13-14, Rev 21:27

[193] Ref 1.3 CCC 1030 - 1032, 1472

[194] Ref 1.1 ESV Matthew 5:48, Malachi 3:2-3, 1 Corinthians 2:12-15

[195] Ref 1.2 RSV 2 Maccabees 12:45, Wisdom 3:1-6

[196] Ref 1.3 CCC 1023 - 1029, 2548

[197] Ref 1.3 CCC 1052

[198] Ref 1.3 CCC 1033 - 1037

[199] Ref 1.1 ESV John 3:16-21, Matthew 25:31-46, John 5:28-29

[200] Ref 1.3 CCC 668 - 682

[201] Ref 1.1 ESV John 14:21, Matthew 25:34-40

[202] Ref 7.14.4 Tim Staples (2021, 11 8). What is Hell? Retrieved from Catholic Answers:
https://www.catholic.com/magazine/online-edition/what-is-hell

[203] Ref 7.14.5 Jim Blackburn (2007, 10 1). Hell? Yes! Retrieved from Catholic Answers:
https://www.catholic.com/magazine/print-edition/hell-yes-part-i

[204] Ref 1.1 ESV 1 Corinthians 15:21, John 14:2-3, 1 Cor 2:9, Matthew 5:8

[205] Ref 7.14.3 Tim Staples (2015, 2 27). What is Heaven? Retrieved from Catholic Answers:
https://www.catholic.com/magazine/online-edition/what-is-heaven

Conclusion

God loves us beyond all measure.

His son, Jesus, was sent to draw us and all of creation into meaningful right relationship. Jesus gave us the Church and the Eucharist; and with the sending of the Holy Spirit, we are guided and sustained in fullness of life, now and into eternity.

We are to live, and draw others into living, in this loving relationship with God and each other - our ultimate fulfillment, now and forever.

Appendix

Structure of the Church

The Church is in vast majority made up of lay persons, i.e., 'the Laity', recognized in the structure or 'order' of things in its own right as a particular state in life and calling (vocation, from the Latin *vocare* – to call). The idea of 'vocation' is often thought of as being reserved to the Ministerial Priesthood and Religious Life as described below, however rightly understood, all the faithful i.e., all of the baptized, are called to live holy lives of faith out in the world - to bring Christ and His love to the world, and the world in love to Christ; being 'salt and light', or 'leaven' are often used images from scripture.

Some of the laity will discern a call to dedicate their lives ("consecrate" – set apart for sacred purpose) to the service of God in a more particular way. A relative few will do so as formally consecrated singles, while the majority of the rest will enter into the Sacrament of Matrimony, i.e., marriage. Alternatively, another category will discern a particular call to serve the faithful via 'ordained' ministry as successors to the first Apostles and their assistants in the context of the Sacrament of Holy Orders. After much discernment, training, and preparation, these individuals enter into the following roles shown in order of progression (though not all proceed through all of the levels):
1) Deacons – assistants to the Priests (Transitional become Priests, Permanent – remain laity)
2) Priests – assistants to the Bishops (alternate titles - Pastor, Monsignor, Parochial Vicar)
3) Bishops – successors to the Apostles (Archbishops cover larger areas and other Bishops)
Note: 'Cardinal' is not a hierarchical position, but an honorary designation.

The Pope is selected from among the world's bishops, and serves as successor to St. Peter, the first 'Vicar of Christ', i.e., 'the prime minister' of the Apostles, the original group of leading ministers. This 'Primacy of Peter', is conveyed to all subsequent Popes (Apostolic Succession) who manifest fatherly leadership of the Church from the jurisdiction of 'the Holy See' (holy chair) in Rome, i.e., The Vatican. The Roman Curia is the administration directly supporting the Pope, and they work together in collegial fashion with all the Bishops of the world.

In addition to the above sacramental holy orders of the diaconate and priesthood (sometimes called 'secular', i.e., "in the world") serving in geographical areas known as 'parishes' within 'dioceses', there are also other groups of individuals consecrated to 'religious life' who generally live in community (some exceptions live in relative isolation, e.g., hermits). While many of these are more visible, living and working in secular settings, others are set apart in community living inside of a convent or monastery. See below "**Religious Life**" for some brief info on a few of these perhaps less visible forms of religious life.

All such orders are outside of the structure of the diocese, and are overseen by a local head individual, who is in turn under the head of the Order. Each Order has a particular character, or 'charism', and therefore a particular purpose or emphasis. Orders are sometimes more readily known by their charism, though many of the founder's lives and legacy are quite extraordinary and also widely known. Individuals in religious life profess vows upon entering into community after an extended and thorough period of discernment and preparation. Some men in religious life are ordained, others are not. They are generally referred to as Brothers (non-ordained), Monks (priests/brothers in monastery), or Friars depending on the order; women religious are generally referred to as Sisters or Nuns.

Religious Life – Examples and Info

1) Benedictines
   a) Solemnity of Saint Benedict of Nursia [https://www.fatherboniface.org/wordpresshome/spiritual-practices/solemnity-of-saint-benedict-of-nursia/]
   b) Monks of Norcia [https://en.nursia.org/]
   c) Shrine of St Walburga [https://stemma.org/shrine-of-st-walburga]
   d) *Gladsome Light - Life in a Byzantine Monastery* [https://www.youtube.com/watch?v=7OJLRt3AZJM]

2) Dominicans
   a) The Thomistic Institute [https://www.youtube.com/c/TheThomisticInstitute/featured]
   b) One Drop of Christ's Blood [https://www.sistersofmary.org/news-events/news/one-drop-of-christs-blood/]

3) Franciscans
   a) About Contemplative Life [https://desertnuns.com/vocation-information/about-the-contemplative-life/]
   b) Franciscan Friars of the Renewal [https://www.franciscanfriars.com/]

he Lord's Prayer - The model prayer; a heartfelt expression of relationship to God and to others [207, 208]

rayed individually, it is an expression of desire in relationship. Prayed in community, it is also an expression of unity, greement. - when two or more gather in my name - agree - It will be done

Matthew 5,6,7 - Sermon on the Mount

9   *Pray then like this:*
     "Our Father in heaven,
          hallowed be your name.
10   *Your kingdom come,*
          your will be done,
     on earth as it is in heaven.
11   *Give us this day our daily bread,*
12   *and forgive us our debts,*
          as we also have forgiven our debtors.
13   *And lead us not into temptation,*
          but deliver us from evil.
          Amen

he Apostles Creed - A concise, comprehensive, and ancient expression of understanding and belief [209]

I believe in God, the Father almighty,
creator of heaven and earth.

I believe in Jesus Christ, his only Son, our Lord.
He was conceived by the power of the Holy Spirit and born of the Virgin Mary.
He suffered under Pontius Pilate,
was crucified, died, and was buried.
He descended to the dead.
On the third day he rose again.
He ascended into heaven,
and is seated at the right hand of the Father.
He will come again to judge the living and the dead.

I believe in the Holy Spirit, the holy catholic Church, the communion of saints, the forgiveness of sins, the resurrection of the body, and the life everlasting. Amen

he Jesus Prayer – simple and fully engaging

"Lord Jesus Christ, Son of God, (breath in)   *have mercy on me, a sinner"* (breath out)

---

[206] 3MC - Episode 68 - What is prayer? (YouTube)
[https://www.youtube.com/watch?v=ED2palqNKa8&index=68&list=PLIcePO_eJb2_EElTdFm1PFLNkH17EQcV-]
[207] Ref 1.1 ESV Matt 6:9-13
[208] Ref 1.3 CCC 2759 - 2865
[209] The Nicene Creed is an expanded version developed later in response to heretical challenges. See Ref 1.3 CCC
     Part 1 – Profession of Faith, pages 49-50 of the USCCB flip-book version online:
[https://www.usccb.org/sites/default/files/flipbooks/catechism/50/]

Other Traditional Prayers: [210]

Hail Mary [211], Glory Be, Guardian Angel prayer, Act of Contrition, Grace before Meals

Devotional Prayers:

Rosary [212], Divine Mercy Chaplet, Angelus, Prayer to St Michael, Litanies [213]

Spontaneous Prayers:

"Thank you Jesus!", "Lord, help me", "Lord, be with me"

Centering prayer

Be with God within, and use a word to stay and return attention to Him.

Center and focus on God alone (Father, Son, Holy Spirit); nothing else, no other.

---

[210] Ref 1.3 USCCB. (2004, November). US Catholic Catechism for Adults. Appendix B (Traditional Prayers)
[https://www.usccb.org/sites/default/files/flipbooks/uscca/files/assets/basic-html/page-560.html]

[211] Elements of this prayer derive from scripture (Ref 1.1 ESV Luke 1:28), Luke 1:42 with a closing petition for intercession.

[212] Ref 9.2 Fr. Mark-Mary (for Ascension Presents). (2019, 10 11). How to REALLY Pray the Rosary. Retrieved from YouTube: [https://www.youtube.com/watch?v=FTd19idM-Jc]

[213] A common misconception is that we pray "to" saints. Properly understood, we pray "thru" saints, asking their intercession.

Reference Materials by Topic, Type

1. **Foundational References** [214]

1.1.   Crossway Bibles. (2001 (Text Edition 2016)). *The Holy Bible, English Standard Version®*. [online via www.biblia.com] Wheaton, IL: Good News Publishers

1.2.   Division of Christian Education of the National Council of Churches of Christ in the United States of America. (New Testament (1965), Old Testament with Apocrypha (1966)). *The Holy Bible, Revised Standard Version Catholic Edition*. [online via www.biblia.com] Wheaton, IL: Good News Publishers

1.3.   Catholic Church. (2016). *Catechism of the Catholic Church* (2nd ed.). [online via https://www.vatican.va/archive/ENG0015/_INDEX.HTM]: United States Catholic Conference.

1.4.   United States Conference of Catholic Bishops (USCCB). (2004, November). United States Catholic Catechism for Adults. Available from USCCB at: [https://www.usccb.org/beliefs-and-teachings/what-we-believe/catechism/us-catholic-catechism-for-adults]

2. **At-a-Glance Summary Materials**

2.1.   D'Ambrosio, M., Cavins, J., & Sri, E. (2020). The Jesus Timeline Chart. West Chester, PA: Ascension Publishing, LLC.

2.2.   Cleaveland, R. R., & (for Our Sunday Visitor, I. (2006). Faith Charts: Catholicism At a Glance. Huntingdon, IN: Our Sunday Visitor Publishing Division.

2.3.   Aquilina, M., & (for Our Sunday Visitor, I. (2010). Faith Charts: The Mass At a Glance. Huntington, IN: Our Sunday Visitor Publishing Division.

2.4.   Hahn, S., & (for Our Sunday Visitor, I. (2008). Faith Charts: The Bible At a Glance. Huntingdon, IN: Our Sunday Visitor Publishing Division.

2.5.   Cavins, J., Gray, T., & Christmyer, S. (2003 (revised 10/04)). Bible Timeline Chart. West Chester, PA: Ascension Press.

3. **Jesus**

3.1.   Pitre, B. (2016). *The Case for Jesus: The Biblical and Historical Evidence for Christ*. New York: Image, an imprint of the Crown Publishing Group (Kindle edition).

3.2.   Strobel, L. (1998 (ePub format)). *The Case for Christ*. Grand Rapids, MI: Zondervan.

3.3.   McDowell, J. (1972, 1979). *Evidence that Demands a Verdict - Volume 1, ebook: Historical Evidences for the Christian Faith*. Here's Life Publishers, Inc. San Bernardino, CA: Thomas Nelson (Kindle Edition).

3.4.   Habermas, G. (2012, 11 8). *The Resurrection Argument That Changed a Generation of Scholars - Gary Habermas at UCSB*. Retrieved from YouTube: [https://www.youtube.com/watch?v=ay_Db4RwZ_M]

3.5.   Kreeft, P. (2008). Jesus-Shock. South Bend, IN: St. Augustine's Press (electronic).

3.6.   C.S.Lewis. (1960). Mere Christianity. New York: Macmillan Publishing Company.

3.7.   G.K.Chesterton. (n.d.). Orthodoxy. Seattle: Amazon Classics (Kindle ebook).

3.8.   Kristen Aebli (for Catholic Exchange). (2017, 9 28). One Thing Adoration. Retrieved from Catholic Exchange: https://catholicexchange.com/one-thing-adoration/

4. **The Church:**

4.1.   Weidenkopf, S., & Schreck, D. A. (2009). Epic: A Journey Through Church History - Chart. West Chester, PA: Ascension Press.

4.2.   Schoeman, R. H. (2003). *Salvation of From the Jews: The Role of Judaism in Salvation History from Abraham to the Second Coming*. San Francisco, CA: Ignatius Press (Kindle edition).

4.3.   Denominations Comparison pamphlet. (2003). Torrance, CA: Rose Publishing, Inc.

4.4.   Levering, M., & Dauphinais, M. (2021). The Wisdom of the Word: Biblical Answers to Ten Pressing Questipons about Catholicicm. Park Ridge IL: Word on Fire Insititute.

---

[214] 'Read the Bible & the Catechism in a Year' Reading Guide [https://chnetwork.org/free-resource-updated-version-of-our-read-the-bible-and-the-catechism-in-a-year-guide/], The Coming Home Network International.

4.5. Moczar, D. (2013). The Church Under Attack: Five Hundred Years That Split the Church and Scattered the Flock. Manchester, NH: Sophia Institute Press.

4.6. Moczar, D. (2010). Seven Lies About Catholic History. Charlotte, NC: TAN Books (Kindle edition).

5.   Tradition:

5.1. Catholic Answers. (1996, (accessed 2022-01-04)). *Pillar of Fire, Pillar of Truth.* Retrieved from Catholic Answers: [https://www.catholic.com/tract/pillar-of-fire-pillar-of-truth]

5.2. St. Philip Institute of Catechesis and Evangelization. (2018). The Way of Christ - Student's Book, First Edition. Tyler, TX: St. Philip Institute of Catechesis and Evangelization.

5.3. St. Philip Institute of Catechesis and Evangelization. (2018). The Way of Christ - Teacher's Guide, First Edition. Tyler, TX: St Philip Institute of Catechesis and Evangelization.

5.4. Barron, F. R. (2011). *Catholicism: A Journey to the Heart of the Faith.* New York, NY: Crown Publishing Group.

5.5. Hahn, S. (1998). A Father Who Keeps His Promises: God's Covenant Love in Scripture. Cincinnati, OH: Servant, an imprint of Franciscan Media.

5.6. USCCB. (2005). *Compendium of the Catechism of the Catholic Church.* USA: United States Conference of Catholic Bishops.

5.7. Aquilina, M., & Stubna, F. K. (1999, 2011). *What Catholics Believe: A Pocket Catechism.* Huntingdon, IN: Our Sunday Visitor Publishing Division (ebook).

5.8. Lukefahr, F. O. (1990, 2nd Edition 1995). "We Believe..." - A Survey of the Catholic Faith, 2nd Edition. Ligouri, MO: Ligouri Publications.

5.9. Therrien, M. (2020). *The Catholic Faith Explained.* Manchester, NH: Sophia Institute Press (eBook).

5.10. Vogt, B. (2017, 2019). *Why I Am Catholic (and You Should Be Too).* Notre Dame, IN: Ave Maria Press (E-book).

5.11. Kaczor, Christopher (for Catholic Answers). (2007, 4 1). *Seven Principals of Catholic Social Teaching.* Retrieved from Catholic Answers: [https://www.catholic.com/magazine/print-edition/seven-principles-of-catholic-social-teaching]

5.12. Beaumont, Douglas M. (for Catholic Answers). (2019, 9 23). *Can Man Become God?* Retrieved from Catholic Answers: [https://www.catholic.com/magazine/online-edition/can-man-become-god]

5.13. Spitzer, F. R. (2017). *Big Book - Credible Catholic.* Retrieved from Credible Catholic: [https://www.crediblecatholic.com/big-book/]

5.14. Horn, T. (2017). Why We're Catholic: Our Reasons for Faith, Hope, and Love. El Cajon, CA: Catholic Answers, Inc (Kindle edition).

6.   Scripture:

6.1. Catholic Biblical Association (Great Britain). (1994). *The Holy Bible: Revised Standard Version, Catholic edition.* USA: National Council of Churches of Christ [online via www.biblia.com].

6.2. Akin, J. (2019). *The Bible is a Catholic Book.* El Cajon, CA: Catholic Answers, Inc.

6.3. The National Catholic Education Commission (NCEC), Australian Catholic Bishops Conference. (n.d.). *Catholic Teaching on Sacred Scripture.* Retrieved from Scripture for Teachers: [https://scripture.catholic.edu.au/index.php/home/foundations/catholic-teaching-on-sacred-scripture/]

6.4. The National Catholic Education Commission (NCEC), Australian Catholic Bishops Conference. (n.d.). *The Principles of Catholic Biblical Scholarship.* Retrieved from Scripture for Teachers: [https://scripture.catholic.edu.au/index.php/home/foundations/catholic-biblical-interpretation/]

6.5. The National Catholic Education Commission (NCEC), Australian Catholic Bishops Conference. (n.d.). *What is a Parable?* Retrieved from Scripture for Teachers: [https://scripture.catholic.edu.au/index.php/home/foundations/what-is-a-parable/]

6.6. Archdiocese of Brisbane, Australia. (2019, 8 12). *The Parable Podcasts,* YouTube Playlist (7 Episodes). Retrieved from Episodes 1: Intro; 2: Prodigal Son; 3: Good Samaritan; 4: Rich Man & Lazarus; 5: Labourers in the Vineyard; 6: The Talents; 7: Great Banquet: [https://www.youtube.com/watch?v=LiEc-Z-J67E&list=PL8-1Dil2Zzb_2SbupaDKZTjyfsY32V7UY]

6.7. The National Catholic Education Commission (NCEC), Australian Catholic Bishops Conference. (n.d.). *The Gospels.* Retrieved from Scripture for Teachers: [https://scripture.catholic.edu.au/index.php/home/foundations/the-gospels/]

6.8. Fr. Mike Schmitz (for Ascension Presents). (2016, 1 12). *Ways to Read the Bible.* Retrieved from YouTube: [https://www.youtube.com/watch?v=6hb7nSL1gKU]

6.9. Fr. Mike Schmitz (for Ascension Presents). (2020, 12 2). *When You Don't Understand the Bible.* Retrieved from YouTube: [https://www.youtube.com/watch?v=FNW-galVANo]

6.10. Saint Joseph Communications. (2010). *Biblical Evidence For Catholics.* Tehachapi, CA: Saint Joseph Communications.

7.   Teaching

7.1. Vatican II documents

7.1.1. Dei verbum (vatican.va) - Dogmatic Constitution on Revelation: [https://www.vatican.va/archive/hist_councils/ii_vatican_council/documents/vat-ii_const_19651118_dei-verbum_en.html]

7.1.2. Lumen Gentium (vatican.va) - Dogmatic Constitution on the Church: [https://www.vatican.va/archive/hist_councils/ii_vatican_council/documents/vat-ii_const_19641121_lumen-gentium_en.html]

7.1.3. Unitatis redintegratio (vatican.va) - Decree on Ecumenism: [https://www.vatican.va/archive/hist_councils/ii_vatican_council/documents/vat-ii_decree_19641121_unitatis-redintegratio_en.html]

7.2.   Fides et Ratio (vatican.va) - Faith and Reason: [https://www.vatican.va/content/john-paul-ii/en/encyclicals/documents/hf_jp-ii_enc_14091998_fides-et-ratio.html]

7.3.   Caritas in veritate (vatican.va) - Charity in Truth: [https://www.vatican.va/content/benedict-xvi/en/encyclicals/documents/hf_ben-xvi_enc_20090629_caritas-in-veritate.html]

7.4.   Veritatis Splendor (vatican.va) - Splendor of Truth: [https://www.vatican.va/content/john-paul-ii/en/encyclicals/documents/hf_jp-ii_enc_06081993_veritatis-splendor.html]

7.5.   Humanae Vitae (vatican.va) - Human Life: [https://www.vatican.va/content/paul-vi/en/encyclicals/documents/hf_p-vi_enc_25071968_humanae-vitae.html]

7.6.   Salvifici Doloris (vatican.va) - Salvific Suffering: [https://www.vatican.va/content/john-paul-ii/en/apost_letters/1984/documents/hf_jp-ii_apl_11021984_salvifici-doloris.html]

7.7.   Deus caritas est (vatican.va) - God is Love: [https://www.vatican.va/content/benedict-xvi/en/encyclicals/documents/hf_ben-xvi_enc_20051225_deus-caritas-est.html]

7.8.   Spe salvi (vatican.va) - In Hope We Are Saved: [https://www.vatican.va/content/benedict-xvi/en/encyclicals/documents/hf_ben-xvi_enc_20071130_spe-salvi.html]

7.9.   Fidei Depositum (vatican.va) – Deposit of Faith: [https://www.vatican.va/content/john-paul-ii/en/apost_constitutions/documents/hf_jp-ii_apc_19921011_fidei-depositum.html]

7.10. Pontifical Biblical Commission to Pope John Paul II on April 23, 1993 - as published in Origins. (1994, 1 6). *The Interpretation of the Bible in the Church.* Retrieved from Catholic Resources.org: [https://catholic-resources.org/ChurchDocs/PBC_Interp.htm]

7.11. Compendium of the Social Doctrine of the Church, Pontifical Council for Justice and Peace (2004, 4 2): [http://www.vatican.va/roman_curia/pontifical_councils/justpeace/documents/rc_pc_justpeace_doc_20060526_compendio-dott-soc_en.html]

7.12. Dives In Misericordia (vatican.va) - God Rich in Mercy: [https://www.vatican.va/content/john-paul-ii/en/encyclicals/documents/hf_jp-ii_enc_30111980_dives-in-misericordia.html]

7.13. Redemptoris Missio (vatican.va) - Mission of the Redeemer: [https://www.vatican.va/content/john-paul-ii/en/encyclicals/documents/hf_jp-ii_enc_07121990_redemptoris-missio.html]

7.14. Teaching - Reference

7.14.1. Akin, J. (2018). *Teaching with Authority: How to Cut Through Doctrinal Confusion & Understand What the Church Really Says.* El Cajon, CA: Catholic Answers Press (Kindle edition)

7.14.2. Jimmy Akin (for Catholic Answers). (2020, 5 30). *A Climb Up the Rungs of Doctrinal Authority.* Retrieved from Catholic Answers: [https://www.catholic.com/magazine/print-edition/a-climb-up-the-rungs-of-doctrinal-authority]

7.14.3. Tim Staples (for Catholic Answers). (2015, 2 27). What is Heaven? Retrieved from Catholic Answers: https://www.catholic.com/magazine/online-edition/what-is-heaven

7.14.4. Tim Staples (for Catholic Answers). (2021, 11 8). What is Hell? Retrieved from Catholic Answers: https://www.catholic.com/magazine/online-edition/what-is-hell

7.14.5. Jim Blackburn (for Catholic Answers). (2007, 10 1). Hell? Yes! Retrieved from Catholic Answers: https://www.catholic.com/magazine/print-edition/hell-yes-part-i

Spiritual Journey

8.1.   Cronin, F. (2020). *The World According to God: The Whole Truth About Life and Living.* Manchester, NH: Sophia Institute Press (Kindle Edition).

8.2.   Trasancos, S. A. (2016). *Particles of Faith: A Catholic Guide to Navigating Science.* Notre Dame, IN: Ave Maria Press (Ebook).

8.2.1. Dr. Stacy Trasancos for (Steubenville Conferences). (2019, 9 27). Dr. Stacy Trasancos - The Faith and Science Conflict Myth (2019 Defending the Faith Conference). Retrieved from YouTube: https://www.youtube.com/watch?v=upAjw3YO7n4

8.3.   Vogt, Brandon (A Claritas U Book). (2020). *What to Say and How to Say It: Discuss Your Catholic Faith with Clarity and Confidence.* Notre Dame, IN: Ave Maria Press (ebook).

8.4.   Vogt, Brandon (A Claritas U Book). (2021). *What to Say and How to Say It: More Ways to Discuss Your Faith with Clarity and Confidence - Volume 2.* Notre Dame, IN: Ave Maria Press (ebook).

8.5.   Martin, R. (2006). *The Fulfillment of All Desire: A Guidebook to God Based on the Wisdom of the Saints.* Steubenville, OH: Emmaus Road Publishing (Kindle Edition).

8.6.   Chautard, J.-B. (1946, 2008). *The Soul of the Apostolate.* Charlotte, NC: TAN Books (Kindle edition)

8.7.   Philippe, Jacques (2007). *Interior Freedom.* New York, NY: Scepter Publishers, Inc.

8.8.   Bishop Robert Barron (for Word on Fire with Brandon Vogt). (2019, 11 11). How to Discern the Spirits. Retrieved from YouTube: [https://www.youtube.com/watch?v=jzYN2hMqLI4]

8.9.   Gallagher, F. T. (n.d.). SD2 A Brief Overview of Rules 1 through 9 – Spiritual Desolation: Be Aware, Understand, Take Action with Fr. Timothy Gallagher – Discerning Hearts Podcast. Retrieved from Discerning Hearts: [

https://www.discerninghearts.com/catholic-podcasts/sd2-a-brief-overview-of-rules-1-through-9-spiritual-desolation-be-aware-understand-take-action-with-fr-timothy-gallagher-discerning-hearts-podcast/]

8.10. One Billion Stories. (2019, 6 19). *Don Briel: a Life of Purpose and Joy*. Retrieved from YouTube: [https://www.youtube.com/watch?v=Xz7qiSeEISc]

8.11. Joseph, M. (2018). *Overwhelming Pursuit: Stop Chasing Your Life and Live*. Huntington, IN: Our Sundy Visitor Publishing Division

8.12. EWTN. (2018). *Icons - 2018-10-26 - Place in Presence*. Retrieved from YouTube: [https://www.youtube.com/watch?v=4hPQEtY_tNw]

8.13. Chris Stefanick (for Real Life Catholic). (2014, 9 30). *You're Kind of a Big Deal*. Retrieved from YouTube: [https://www.youtube.com/watch?v=d_34gjdHp3M]

8.14. Centricity Worship. (2014, 9 15). Lauren Daigle - "Come Alive (Dry Bones) (Live at the CentricWorship Retreat). Retrieved from YouTube: [https://www.youtube.com/watch?v=7XAeyFagceQ]

8.15. Gumbel, N. (1993, 1996, 2003, 2010, 2016). Questions of Life. Nashville, TN: W Publishing Group (eBook).

8.16. Ortberg, J. (2005). God is Closer Than You Think. Grand Rapids, MI: Zondervan (Kindle Edition)

8.17. Adam Blai (for EWTN). (2016, 01 02). *EWTN On Location - Exorcism In The Modern Church And How To Keep The Doors To The Demonic Closed*. Retrieved from YouTube: [https://www.youtube.com/watch?v=JKnGdr9WMqs]

8.18. Tadié, S. (2020, 9 29). Renowned Angel Expert Explains Amazing Facts Every Catholic Should Know About Angels. Retrieved from National Catholic Register (ncregister.com): [https://www.ncregister.com/blog/angels-101]

8.19. FrassatiUSA. (2016, 4 17). PGF (Per Giorgio Frassati) get to know him TEASER. Retrieved from YouTube: https://www.youtube.com/watch?v=bagWsNLOl0I&

8.20. HM Television (English). (2016, 11 14). All or Nothing: Sr. Clare Crockett - Official Trailer. Retrieved from YouTube: https://www.youtube.com/watch?v=N7sBW-cnWgA

9.   Prayer:

9.1. Acklin, F. T., & Hicks, F. B. (2019). *Personal Prayer: A Guide for Receiving the Father's Love*. Steubenville, OH: Emmaus Road Publishing (Kindle edition).

9.2. Fr. Mark-Mary (for Ascension Presents). (2019, 10 11). *How to REALLY Pray the Rosary*. Retrieved from YouTube: [https://www.youtube.com/watch?v=FTd19idM-Jc]

9.3. Hallow – prayer and meditation app [https://hallow.com]

9.4. Meditation – "I Shall Keep the Silence of My Heart" [pages 507-508, from Mother Teresa, cited in 'The Power of Prayer' (New York: MJF Books, 1998)]. Retrieved from USCCB Flipbook - United States Catholic Catechism for Adults: [https://www.usccb.org/sites/default/files/flipbooks/uscca/files/assets/basic-html/page-507.html]

9.5. Catholic-Link. (n.d.). *Gallery: 10 Ways to Pray*. Retrieved from Catholic Resources from Catholic-Link: [https://catholic-link.org/images/gallery-10-ways-to-pray/]

9.6. United States Conference of Catholic Bishops. (n.d.). *Prayer | USCCB*. Retrieved from USCCB: [https://www.usccb.org/prayer-and-worship/prayers-and-devotions/prayers]

9.7. Stevers, D. (n.d.). *Dan Stevers - Prayer Intro - YouTube*. Retrieved from YouTube: [https://www.youtube.com/watch?v=C5S2flwltts&list=PLtS8Xw9v7kRdp4brbPAo9HoDhCnEakIxx&index=2]

9.8. National Catholic Register. (n.d.). *Tag 'lectio divina' - NCRegister*. Retrieved from National Catholic Register: [https://www.ncregister.com/tag/lectio-divina]

9.9. United Conference of Catholic Bishops. (n.d.). *Meditations | USCCB*. Retrieved from USCCB: [https://www.usccb.org/prayer-and-worship/prayers-and-devotions/meditations]

9.10. Benedictines of Mary, Queen of Apostles, *The Hearts of Jesus, Mary & Joseph at Ephesus*. Retrieved from YouTube: [https://www.youtube.com/playlist?list=OLAK5uy_IKKvvOD_8YupOiiLE6Ld6SW00DmoSwL3o]

10.   Worship:

10.1. Sri, E. (2011). *A Biblical Walk Through the Mass: Understanding What We Say and Do in the Liturgy*. West Chester, PA: Assension Press (Kindle edition).

10.2. Burke-Sivers, D. H. (2012). *The Mass in Sacred Scripture*. Portland, OR: Aurem Cordis Publications (Kindle Edition).

10.3. Barron, B. R. (2020, 02 27). *The Real Presence of Jesus in the Eucharist // Bishop Barron at 2020 Religious Education Congress*. Retrieved from YouTube: [https://www.youtube.com/watch?v=UzCPu_IEhe8]

10.4. Dr. Ray Guarendi. (2020, 11 16). *Why Be Catholic? | Full Movie*, segment on the Eucharist – The Quarter (29:40 – 35:41) Retrieved from YouTube: [https://www.youtube.com/embed/faZV--bkiGY?start=1919&end=2141]

10.5. Carstens, C. (2017). *A Devotional Journey Into the Mass: How Mass Can Become a Time of Grace, Nourishment, and Devotion*. Manchester, NH: Sophia Institute Press.

10.6. Much more...

10.7. Scalia, E. (2018). The Mass - Study Guide: A Catholic Study Program presented by Most Rev. Robert E. Barron. Word on Fire Catholic Ministries.

11.   Miracles:

11.1. O'Neill, M. (Copyright 2015 (accessed 2022-01-04)). *The Miracle Hunter*. Retrieved from The Miracle Hunter: [http://miraclehunter.com/]

11.2.   Spitzer, R. J. (2010). New Proofs for the Existence of God: Contributions of Contemporary Physics and Philosophy. Grand Rapids, MI: Wm. B. Eerdmans Publishing Co. (Kindle edition).

11.3.   Schuchts, B. (2014). Be Healed: A Guide to Encountering the Powerful Love of Jesus in Your Life. Notre Dame, IN: Ave Maria Press.

11.4.   O'Neill, M. (2022). Science and the Miraculous: How the Church Investigates the Supernatural. Charlotte, NC: TAN Books.

2.   General:

12.1.   Winseman, A. L., Clifton, D. O., & Liesveld, C. (2003, 2004, 2008). Living Your Strengths: Discover Your God-Given Talents and Inspire Your Community. New York, NY: Gallup Press (Kindle edition).

12.2.   Rath, T. (2007, 2015). StrengthsFinder 2.0. New York, NY: Gallup Press (Kindle edition).

TWTTTL

46

Resource Lists

Media Platforms and Programming

) Acts XXIX [https://www.actsxxix.org]; 1050 Porter St., Detroit, MI 48226; (313) 315-3320; [info@actsxxix.org]
   a) "Someone has Come to Fight" | The Kerygma | Fr. John Riccardo – YouTube [https://www.youtube.com/watch?v=XqafKxFiktQ]
) Ahava Productions;
   P.O. Box 393, Oconomowoc, WI 53066; [https://www.ahavaproductions.com/contact]
   a) ANIMA – a three-part production on the life of faith (Crux, Kenosis, Blaze) [https://www.ahavaproductions.com/anima]
   b) ECHO – a video presentation of the US Catholic Catechism for Adults (Ref 1.3) in 36 short (3-5 min) segments (listing below)
      http://www.ahavaproductions.com/echo/
      ECHO-00_Ahava_Promo

ECHO-01_1_Creed_I_My Soul Longs for You O God	ECHO-19_2_Sacraments_XIX_Anointing the Sick and the Dying
ECHO-02_1_Creed_II_God Comes to Meet Us	ECHO-20_2_Sacraments_XX_Holy Orders
ECHO-03_1_Creed_III_Proclaim the Gospel to Every Creature	ECHO-21_2_Sacramentrs_XXI_The Sacrament of Marriage
ECHO-04_1_Creed_IV_Bring about the Obedience of Faith	ECHO-22_2_Sacraments_XXII Sacramentals, Popular Devotions
ECHO-05_1_Creed_V_I Believe in God	ECHO-23_3_Morality_XXIII Life in Christ - Part One
ECHO-06_1_Creed_VI_Man and Woman in the Beginning	ECHO-24_3_Morality_XXIV Life In Christ - Part Two
ECHO-07_1_Creed_VII_The Good News - God has sent His Son	ECHO-25_3_Morality_XXV 1st Commandment-Believe in True God
ECHO-08_1_Creed_VIII_The Saving Death - Resurrection of Christ	ECHO-26_3_Morality_XXVI 2nd Commandment-Reverence Name
ECHO-09_1_Creed_IX_Receive the Holy Spirit	ECHO-27_3_Morality_XXVII 3rd Commandment-Love Lord's Day
ECHO-10_1_Creed_X_The Church - Reflecting the Light of Christ	ECHO-28_3_Morality_XXVIII 4th Commandment-Strengthen Family
ECHO-11_1_Creed_XI_The Four Marks of the Church	ECHO-29_3_Morality_XXIX 5th Commandment-Promote Life
ECHO-12_1_Creed_XII_Mary - Church's 1st,Most Perfect Member	ECHO-30_3_Morality_XXX 6th Commandment-Marital Fidelity
ECHO-13_1_Creed_XIII_Our Eternal Destiny	ECHO-31_3_Morality_XXXI 7th Commandment-Do Not Steal
ECHO-14_1_Creed_XIV_Celebration of the Pascal Mystery of Christ	ECHO-32_3_Morality_XXXII 8th Commandment-Tell the Truth
ECHO-15_2_Sacraments_XV_Baptism - Becoming a Christian	ECHO-33_3_Morality_XXXIII 9th Commandment-Purity of Heart
ECHO-16_2_Sacraments_XVI Confirmation-Consecrated - Mission	ECHO-34_3_Morality_XXXIX 10th Commandment-Poverty of Spirit
ECHO-17_2_Sacraments_XVII_The Eucharist - Source and Summit	ECHO-35_4_Prayer_XXXV God Calls Us to Pray
ECHO-18_2_Sacraments_XVIII_Sacrament of Reconciliation-Mercy	ECHO-36_4_Prayer_XXXVI Jesus Taught Us to Pray

) Augustine Institute – FORMED [https://formed.org]
   6160 S Syracuse Way - Suite 310, Greenwood Village, CO 80111, (303) 937-4420; [info@augustineinstitute.org]
   a) Symbolon [https://watch.formed.org/symbolon-the-catholic-faith-explained]
   b) The Search [https://watch.formed.org/products/the-search-begins-full-series]
) Ascension Press [https://ascensionpress.com];
   PO Box 1990, West Chester, PA 19380; 1-484-875-4550; [support@ascensionpress.com]
   a) Great Adventure Bible Study [https://ascensionpress.com/pages/the-great-adventure]
   b) Bible in a Year podcast [https://media.ascensionpress.com/all-bible-in-a-year-episodes/]
   c) Bible in a Year reading guide [https://ascensionpress.com/pages/biy-registration]
   d) Catechism in a Year Podcast [https://ascensionpress.com/pages/catechisminayear]
   e) Chosen [https://ascensionpress.com/collections/chosen-this-is-your-catholic-faith%20]
   f) You [https://ascensionpress.com/collections/you-life-love-and-the-theology-of-the-body]
) Catholic Answers [https://www.catholic.com];
   2020 Gillespie Way, El Cajon, CA 92020; (619) 387-7200; [media@catholic.com]
) ClaritasU [https://www.claritasu.com]; [support@claritasu.com]
") Dynamic Catholic [https://www.dynamiccatholic.com/];
   5081 Olympic Blvd., Erlanger, KY 41018; (859) 980-7900; [info@dynamiccatholic.com]
) EWTN Global Catholic Television Network [https://www.ewtn.com];
   5817 Old Leeds Rd., Irondale, Alabama 35210; 1-800-447-3986; [viewer@ewtn.com]
   a) Crossing the Goal [http://www.crossingthegoal.com/workout-groups/content-lineup/team-sfw]

b) On Demand [https://ondemand.ewtn.com/]
c) Fr Spitzer's Universe [https://ondemand.ewtn.com/free/Home/Series/ondemand/video/en/fr-spitzers-universe]
d) Icons [https://ondemand.ewtn.com/free/Home/Series/ondemand/video/en/icons]
e) Journey Home [https://ondemand.ewtn.com/free/Home/Series/ondemand/video/en/the-journey-home]
f) Scripture and Tradition [https://ondemand.ewtn.com/free/Home/Series/ondemand/video/en/scripture-and-tradition]
g) The Wonders of His Mercy, Fr Wade Menezes – Episode 4: THE 14 WORKS OF MERCY
[https://www.youtube.com/watch?v=kJyDWhg9390]
h) The Heresies [https://ondemand.ewtn.com/paid/Home/Series/catalog/video/en/the-heresies]
i) "Lives of Saints", Published by John J. Crawley & Co., Inc. - excerpt via EWTN website. (n.d.). *Saint Paul, Apostle to the Gentiles*. Retrieved from EWTN Global Catholic Television Network: Catholic News, TV, Radio | EWTN: [https://www.ewtn.com/catholicism/library/saint-paul-apostle-to-the-gentiles-5731]
j) "Lives of Saints", Published by John J. Crawley & Co., Inc. - excerpt via EWTN website. (n.d.). *Saint Peter, Prince of the Apostles*. Retrieved from EWTN Global Catholic Television Network: Catholic News, TV, Radio | EWTN: [https://www.ewtn.com/catholicism/library/saint-peter-prince-of-the-apostles-5749]

9) Franciscan University of Steubenville; [https://franciscan.edu/]
1235 University Blvd., Steubenville, Ohio 43952; (740) 284-5893; [presents@franciscan.edu]
a) Franciscan Presents [https://www.faithandreason.com/franciscan-university-presents]
b) The Wild Goose [https://wildgoose.tv/]
c) Metanoia [https://wildgoose.tv/]

10) Magis Center [https://magiscenter.com/];
Christ Cathedral Tower-Ninth Floor, 13280 Chapman Avenue, Garden Grove, CA 92840; (949) 271-2727 ext. 4
a) Credible Catholic [https://www.crediblecatholic.com/]
b) Purposeful Universe [http://www.purposefuluniverse.com/]

11) Miracle Hunter [http://miraclehunter.com/]; [questions@miraclehunter.com]
a) Discernment [http://miraclehunter.com/marian_apparitions/discernment/]
b) Miracles (Apparitions, Images, Eucharistic, Stigmata, Incorruptibles) [http://miraclehunter.com/miracles/]
c) Videos [http://miraclehunter.com/tv/index.html]
d) Books [http://miraclehunter.com/books/]
i) O'Neill, M. (2021). *They Might Be Saints: On the Path to Sainthood in America*. Irondale, Alabama: EWTN Publishing, Inc.

12) Real Life Catholic; [https://reallifecatholic.com/] 6160 S. Syracuse Way, Ste 100, Greenwood Village, CO 80111; 330-732-5228; [info@reallifecatholic.com]
a) Real Life Catholic - YouTube [https://www.youtube.com/channel/UC9Gin8zVjjzywF_sW9fkODA]
b) Real Life Catholic - Holy Dirt [https://www.facebook.com/ewtnonline/videos/real-life-catholic-holy-dirt/10154797804202582/]

13) St Paul Center [https://stpaulcenter.com/];
1468 Parkview Circle Steubenville, OH 43952; 740-264-9535; [customerservice@stpaulcenter.com]

14) St Philip Institute [https://stphilipinstitute.org/];
1015 ESE Loop 323 Tyler, Texas 75701-9663; (903) 630-5055; info@stphilipinstitute.org
a) The Way of Christ [https://stphilipinstitute.org/christian-initiation/]
b) Christian Initiation Catechism: A Guide for Children and Families
[https://stphilipinstitute.square.site/product/christian-initiation-catechism-a-guide-for-children-and-families/75?cp=true&sa=false&sbp=false&q=false&category_id=3]

15) WAOB - We Are One Body® Radio Network; [https://www.waob.org/]
1100 Ligonier Street, Suite 305Latrobe, PA 15650; [web@waob.org]

16) Word on Fire [https://www.wordonfire.org/];
P.O. Box 170, Des Plaines, IL 60016; 866-928-1237 ext. 1; [contact@wordonfire.org]
a) Barron, F. R. (2011). *Catholicism: A Journey to the Heart of the Faith*. New York, NY: Crown Publishing Group.
b) Catholicism (DVD and study materials)
[https://bookstore.wordonfire.org/products/catholicism-series-leaders-kit]
c) Bishop Robert Barron (for Word On Fire). (2015). *Untold Blessing: Three Paths to Holiness* (DVD and study materials). USA. https://bookstore.wordonfire.org/collections/untold-blessing]

Publishers

17) Ignatius Press [https://www.ignatius.com/];
1348 10TH Ave., San Francisco, CA 94122; 1-888-615-3186; [info@ignatius.com]
18) Sophia Institute Press [https://www.sophiainstitute.com/];
P.O. Box 5284, Manchester, NH 03108; (800) 888-9344; [CustomerService@SophiaInstitute.com]
19) TAN Books [https://tanbooks.com/]

Apostolates

20) Aid to the Church in Need [https://www.churchinneed.org/];
725 Leonard Street, P.O. Box 220384, Brooklyn, NY 11222; (800) 628-6333; [info@churchinneed.org]
21) Catholics Come Home [https://www.catholicscomehome.org/]; PO Box 1802, Roswell, GA 30077

2) CENEWA [https://cnewa.org/]; 1011 1st Ave, Floor 15, New York, NY 10022-4195; (212) 826-1480
3) Encounter Ministries [https://encounterministries.us/];
730 Rickett Rd., Brighton, MI 48116; mail@encounterministries.us
   a) Fearless documentary [https://www.fearlessdocumentary.net/]
4) FOCUS – Fellowship of Catholic University Students [https://www.focus.org/];
603 Park Point Dr., Golden, CO 80401; 303.962.5750; info@focus.org
5) Hard as Nails Ministries [https://www.amazingnation.org/]; 905 7th North St., Liverpool, NY 13088; (888) 498-2255
   a) ABC Justin Fatica HANM interview with Dan Harris [https://www.youtube.com/watch?v=L38rwpU_4Rk&list=PL-UqJ3ASAgHg2E1ep7xPp79vPfs-KBe1W&index=10]
6) John Paul II Healing Center [https://jpiihealingcenter.org/];
2910 Kerry Forest Pkwy #D4-344, Tallahassee, FL 32309; [info@jpiihealingcenter.org]
   a) Be Healed, Dr. Bob Schuchts [https://jpiihealingcenter.org/product/be-healed-dr-bob-schuchts-copy/]
7) Dr. Allen Hunt [https://drallenhunt.com/]
   a) Hunt, D. A. (2014, 3 22). Charlotte Catholic Men's Conference 2014 - Dr. Allen Hunt. Retrieved from YouTube - Dan Trapini: https://www.youtube.com/watch?v=S8OYTFKrH40
8) MTYR - You are More Than You Realize [https://mtyr.org/]; an initiative of Preambula Group [https://preambula.org/contact/]
9) Steve Ray [https://catholicconvert.com/]; [sray@me.com]
10) Renewal Ministries [https://www.renewalministries.net/];
PO Box 491 · Ann Arbor, MI 48106; (734) 662-1730; [reception@renewalministries.net]
11) Deacon Harold Burke-Sivers [https://deaconharold.com/]
   a) Burke-Sivers, D. H. (2016, 8 24). Deacon Harold Burke-Sivers - Gathering of Catholic Men 2015. Retrieved from YouTube: [https://www.youtube.com/watch?v=nbU8ZeileOY]
12) The Ark and the Dove, 10745 Babcock Boulevard, Gibsonia, PA 15044; (724) 444-8055; info@TheArkAndTheDoveWorldwide.org [https://www.thearkandthedoveworldwide.org/en/]
13) The Coming Home Network International; [https://chnetwork.org]; P.O. Box 8290, Zanesville, OH 43702; 740-450-1175
14) The Culture Project; [https://thecultureproject.org/]; P.O. Box 86, Wynnewood, PA 19096; 1 (800) 315 8684; [info@thecultureproject.org]
15) The Vigil Project [https://www.thevigilproject.com/]
   a) What A Beautiful Name feat. John Finch by The Vigil Project | Live At The Steeple - YouTube [https://www.youtube.com/watch?v=k5VOjA_wr4w&list=PLL3qLwUv0EKaLQGut_NTHiLBCaGocGXkc&index=2]
   b) In Need of a Savior // feat. Andrea Thomas #VIGIL - YouTube [https://www.youtube.com/watch?v=1LEj4LPCcgM]

Blogs, Podcasts, and Notables
16) Intellectual Takeout blog [https://www.intellectualtakeout.org/]
17) Peter Kreeft blog [https://peterkreeft.com/books.htm]
18) Pints with Aquinas, Matt Fradd [https://pintswithaquinas.com/]
19) Counsel of Trent, Trent Horn [https://www.catholic.com/audio/cot]
20) You Were Born for This, Fr. John Riccardo [You Were Born for This Podcast — ACTS XXIX]
21) Luke 24 - Steve Wood [https://luke21radio.podbean.com/]
22) Keenen Kampa, Ballerina – Jerome Lejeune Foundation USA [https://lejeunefoundation.org/team/keenan-kampa/]
   a) Catholic Ballerina Dances With Added Purpose in 'High Strung'| National Catholic Register [https://www.ncregister.com/news/catholic-ballerina-dances-with-added-purpose-in-high-strung]
   b) Venerable Jerome Lejeune, To the Least of These my Brothers & Sisters – YouTube [https://www.youtube.com/watch?v=PKJbUUXWT4s]
23) Jennifer Fulwiler, radio show host, stand-up comedian, author
   a) Convinced EP. 1 [http://convincedcatholic.org/2019/07/jennifer-fulwiler-conversion-story/]
   b) Fulwiler, J. (2014). Something Other Than God: How I Passionately Sought Happiness and Accidentally Found It. San Francisco, CA: Ignatius Press.
24) Roy Schoeman, Jewish convert, former Harvard professor, MIT undergrad
   a) Schoeman, R. (2020, 01 07). "From Jewish Harvard Professor to Catholic Evangelist". Retrieved from YouTube: [https://www.youtube.com/watch?v=Enr-iLahEl4]
25) Novak, M. (1982, 1991). The Spirit of Democratic Capitalism. New York, NY: Madison Books (Kindle edition).
26) Schuchts, B. (2014). Be Healed: A Guide to Encountering the Powerful Love of Jesus in Your Life. Notre Dame, IN: Ave Maria Press.
27) Widmer, A. (2022). The Art of Principled Entrepreneurship. Dallas, TX: BenBella Books, Inc.

TWTTTL

Saints

Saints A to Z – Catholic Online [https://www.catholic.org/saints/stindex.php] > (selected notables below)
Saint of the Day – [https://www.youtube.com/playlist?list=PL58g24NgWPlzvBk2IQVES_xC4WTm6-CDI]
Albert the Great [https://www.catholic.org/saints/saint.php?saint_id=144]

For below Saints, use the same web URL as show above for Albert the Great, but substitute the noted 'id' a
shown.
Links to full-length films are provided where available [T – trailer, F – Formed, I – Ignatius Press].

- Alphonsus Liguori [1284]
- Ambrose [16]
- Andrew [109]
- Anthony of Padua [24]
- Anthony the Abbot [23]
- Augustine [418] [T, F]
- Bakita [5601] [T, F]
- Barbara [166] [T, F]
- Bartholomew [390]
- Basil [261]
- Bede [574]
- Benedict [26]
- Benedict the Moor [871]
- Bernadette [147] {T, F]
- Bernard of Clairvaux [559]
- Blaise [28]
- Bonaventure 169]
- Bonafice of Mainz [29]
- Catherine of Siena [9]
- Catherine Laboure [266]
- Charbel [112]
- Clare [215] [T, F]
- Cyril of Alexandria [616]
- Cyril of Jerusalem [40]
- Damian of Molokai [2817]
- Dominic [178]
- Edith Stein [179]
- Ephrem [3]
- Elizabeth Seton [180]
- Faustina [510]
- Francis [50] [T, F]
- Francis de Sales [51]
- Francis Xavier [423]
- Fulton Sheen (Venerable) [7731]
- Gabriel [279]
- Gemma Galgiani [225]
- Giana Molla [6985]
- Gregory the Great [54]
- Helena [123]
- Hildegard of Bingen [3777]
- Ignatius of Antioch [677]
- Ignatius of Loyola [56] [T, I]
- Irenaeus [291]
- Isaac Jogues [151]
- Isidore of Seville [58]
- James the Greater [59]
- James the Lesser [356]
- Jerome [10]
- John [228]
- Joan of Arc [295] [T, F]
- John Bosco [63] [T, F]
- John Chrysostom [64]
- John Henry Newman [46073]
- John of the Cross [65]
- John Paul II [6996] [T, F]
- John Vianney [399]
- Joseph [4]
- Jose Louis Sanchez del Rio [46079]
- Juan Diego [73]
- Thaddaeus [127]
- Junipero Serra [401]
- Justin Martyr [4144]
- Kateri Tekakwitha [154]
- Kathryn Drexel [193]
- Lawrence [366]
- Leo the Great [299]
- Louis de Montfort [458]
- Luke [76]
- Mark [305]
- Maria Goretti [78]
- Matthew [84]
- Maximillan Kolbe [370]
- Miguel Pro (Blessed) [86]
- Michael [308]
- Monica [1]
- Mother Cabrini [278]
- Mother Teresa [5611] [T, F]
- Nicholas [371]
- Padre Pio [311] [T, F]
- Patrick [89]
- Paul [91]
- Per Georgio Frassati (Blessed) [6994]
- Peter [5358] [T, F]
- Peter Canisius [93]
- Peter Damian [780]
- Philip Neri [97] [T, F]
- Phillip [312]
- Polycarp [99] [T]
- Raphael [203]
- Rita [205] [F]
- Robert Bellarmine [101]
- Simon [241]
- Solanus Casey (Venerable) [382]
- Stephen [137]
- Teresa of Avila [208]
- Therese of Lisieux [105]
- Thomas [410]
- Thomas Aquinas [2530]
- Thomas Becket [12]
- Thomas More [324]
- Timothy [367]
- Vincent de Paul [326]

Notes

Made in the USA
Columbia, SC
02 August 2022